People weekly

YEARBOOK

THE YEAR IN REVIEW: 1995

Published by

A division of Time Inc. Home Entertainment
1271 Avenue of the Americas
New York, NY 10020

PEOPLE WEEKLY is a registered trademark of Time Inc.
ISBN: 1-883013-32-1
Manufactured in the United States of America

PEOPLE YEARBOOK 1996

EDITOR: Richard Burgheim

SENIOR WRITER: David Grogan

ART DIRECTOR: Anthony Kosner

PICTURE EDITOR: Patricia Cadley

CHIEF OF RESEARCH: Denise Lynch

COPY EDITOR: Ricki Tarlow

OPERATIONS: Charles Castillo

Special thanks to Alan Anuskiewicz, Khalif Bobatoon, Robert Britton, Steven Cook, Deirdre Cossman, Beth Filler, Brien Foy, Michelle Green, Penny M. Hays, George Hill, Nancy Houghtaling, Anne Kilpatrick, Mary Carroll Marden, Elsa Mehary, Eric Mischel, James Mittelmark, James Oberman, J. D. Reed, Matthew Semble, Elizabeth Sporkin, Eileen Sweet, Susan Toepfer, Maria Tucci, Mindy Viola, Roger Wolmuth, Liz Zale and, for the introductory essay, Richard Lacayo.

PEOPLE CONSUMER MARKETING
VICE PRESIDENT: Jeremy Koch
CIRCULATION DIRECTOR: Greg Harris
ASST. CONSUMER MARKETING DIRECTOR: Bill Barber
MARKETING MANAGER: Maureen O'Brien

TIME INC. NEW BUSINESS DEVELOPMENT
DIRECTOR: David Gitow
ASSOCIATE DIRECTOR: H. Stuart Hotchkiss
ASSISTANT DIRECTOR: Peter Shapiro
FULFILLMENT DIRECTOR: Mary Warner McGrade
DEVELOPMENT MANAGER: John Sandklev
DEVELOPMENT MANAGER: Robert Fox
OPERATIONS MANAGER: John Calvano
PRODUCTION MANAGER: Donna Miano-Ferrara
ASSOC. DEVELOPMENT MANAGER: Mike Holahan
ASST. DEVELOPMENT MANAGER: Allison Weiss
ASST. DEVELOPMENT MANAGER: Dawn Weland
MARKETING ASSISTANT: Charlotte Siddiqui

TIME INC. MAGAZINES
EDITOR-IN-CHIEF: Norman Pearlstine
EDITORIAL DIRECTOR: Henry Muller
EDITOR OF NEW MEDIA: Walter Isaacson

TIME INC.
CHAIRMAN: Reginald K. Brack Jr.
PRESIDENT, CEO: Don Logan

PEOPLE YEARBOOK REFLECTS THE EFFORTS OF THE EDITORIAL STAFF OF *PEOPLE WEEKLY*

MANAGING EDITOR Landon Y. Jones Jr.
DEPUTY MANAGING EDITOR Carol Wallace
EXECUTIVE EDITORS Cutler Durkee, Susan Toepfer
ASSISTANT MANAGING EDITORS Ross Drake, Charles Leerhsen, Hal Wingo (International), Roger R. Wolmuth, Jacob Young
EDITOR, SPECIAL PROJECTS Eric Levin
CHIEF OF CORRESPONDENTS Joe Treen
SENIOR WRITERS Marilyn Balamaci (News), Hugh Delehanty, Jack Friedman, Susan Hornik, Bonnie Johnson, Barbara Kantrowitz, Jack Kelley (Los Angeles), Kristin McMurran, Mari McQueen, Ralph Novak, Joseph Poindexter, Elizabeth Sporkin
ART DIRECTOR John Shecut Jr.
PICTURE EDITOR Mary Carroll Marden
CHIEF OF REPORTERS Nancy Pierce Williamson
CHIEF OF STAFF Sarah Brody
ASSOCIATE EDITORS Thomas Fields-Meyer, Michelle Green, Kim Hubbard, Michael A. Lipton, J.D. Reed, Leah Rozen, Karen S. Schneider
SENIOR WRITERS Peter Castro, Gregory Cerio, Steven Dougherty, Tom Gliatto, David Grogan, Bill Hewitt, David Hiltbrand, Richard Jerome, Pam Lambert, Shelley Levitt, Michael J. Neill, William Plummer, Jill Rachlin, Susan K. Reed, Curtis Rist, Marjorie Rosen, Cynthia Sanz, Susan Schindehette
STAFF WRITERS Kim Cunningham, Eileen Daspin, David Ellis, Kevin Gray, Dan Jewel, Janice Min, J.D. Podolsky, Patrick Rogers, Joyce Wansley
WRITER-REPORTERS Andrew Abrahams (Deputy Chief), Veronica Burns, Denise Lynch (Deputies, Special Projects), Lisa Kay Greissinger, Lorna Grisby, Mary S. Huzinec, Toby Kahn, Allison Lynn, Sabrina McFarland, Irene Kubota Neves, Lisa Russell, Maria Speidel
REPORTERS David Cobb Craig, Ann Guerin, Jeremy Helligar, Averie LaRussa, Hugh McCarten, Erik Meers, Lan N. Nguyen, Gail Nussbaum, Vincent R. Peterson, Mary Shaughnessy, Ying Sita, Genevieve A. Smith, Brooke Bizzell Stachyra, Leslie Strauss, Jane Sugden, Randy Vest, Cynthia Wang, Robin Ward
RESEARCH OPERATIONS James Oberman (Manager), Matthew Semble, Robert Britton, Steven Cook
PICTURE DEPARTMENT Beth Filler (Deputy), Mary Fanette, Holly Holden, Maddy Miller, Sarah Rozen (Associate Editors), Lynn Bernstein, Suzanne Cheruk, Anne Kilpatrick, Mary Ellen Lidon, Eileen Sweet, Freyda Tavin, Mindy Viola, Blanche Williamson (Assistant Editors), Stan J. Williams (Picture Desk), Michael Brandson, Tom Mattie, Karin Grant (Los Angeles), Jerene Jones (London)
ART DEPARTMENT Hilli Pitzer (Deputy Director), Phil Simone (Special Projects Director), Helene Elek (Associate Director), Angela Alleyne (Assistant Director), Tom Allison, Ronnie Brandwein, Mary M. Hauck (Designers), Sal Argenziano, Allan D. Bintliff Sr., Brien Foy, Joseph Randazzo
COPY DESK Nancy Houghtaling (Chief), David Greisen, Patricia R. Kornberg (Deputies), Will Becker, Judith I. Fogarty, Rose Kaplan (Copy Coordinators), Hollis C. Bernard, William Doares, Amalia Duarte, Ben Harte, Alan Levine, Mary C. Radich, Muriel C. Rosenblum, Sheryl F. Stein (Copy Editors), Lillian Nici, Deborah Ratel, Patricia Rommeney, Joanann Scali (Assistants)
OPERATIONS Alan Anuskiewicz (Manager), Anthony M. Zarvos (Deputy), Michael G. Aponte, Soheila Asayesh, Donna Cheng, Denise M. Doran, George W. Hill, Michelle Lockhart, Key Martin, Elsabeth Mehary, Mia Rublowska, Ellen Shapiro, Larry Whiteford
TECHNOLOGY Tom Klein (Director), James Mittelmark (Deputy Director), Janie Greene, Fred Kao, Eric Mischel, Gregory Paik, Alison Sawyer, Stephanie Wedra
PRODUCTION Robert Bronzo, Paul Castrataro, Thomas C. Colaprico, Geri Flanagan, Paul Zelinski (Managers), Catherine Barron, Kalen Donaldson, Karen J. Waller, Anthony White
IMAGING Betsy Castillo (Manager), Paul Dovell, Robert Fagan, Francis Fitzgerald, Patricia Fitzgerald Gordon, Kevin Grimstead, Henry Groskinsky, Kin Wah Lam, James M. Lello, Brian Luckey, Anthony G. Moore, David Pandy, Susan Power, Joanne Recca, Robert Roszkowski, Randall Swift, Warren Thompson, Peter Tylus, Susan Vroom
DIRECTOR, NEW MEDIA Hala Makowska
NEW MEDIA DEPARTMENT Mary H.J. Farrell (Editor, People Online), Lorraine Goods
PUBLIC AFFAIRS Susan Ollinick (Director), Dianne Jones, Sheri Wohl Lapidus, Akieva Harrell
EDITORIAL BUSINESS MANAGER Maria Tucci, Orpha Davis (Deputy)
ADMINISTRATION Susan Baldwin, Bernard Acquaye, Isabel Alves, Nancy Eils, Rayna L. Evans, Joy Fordyce, Deirdre Gallagher, Mercedes Mitchell, Marie L. Parker, Jean Reynolds, Shirley Van Putten, Martha White, Maureen S. Fulton (Letters/Syndication Manager)
NEWS BUREAU Elizabeth F. McNeil, William Brzozowski, Bonnie J. Smith, Richard G. Williams
NATIONAL CORRESPONDENT Lois Armstrong
DOMESTIC BUREAUS CHICAGO, Giovanna Breu (Chief), Bryan Alexander, Luchina Fisher, Julie Greenwalt, Leisa Marthaler; HOUSTON, Anne Maier; LOS ANGELES, Todd Gold (Deputy Chief), Lorenzo Benet, Karen Brailsford, Betty Cortina, Thomas Cunneff, Johnny Dodd, John Hannah, Kristina Johnson, Vicki Sheff-Cahan, Lyndon Stambler, Craig Tomashoff, Lynda Wright, Paula Yoo, Florence Nishida, Monica Rizzo, Kenneth A. Baker, Monica Clark; MIAMI, Meg Grant (Chief), Cindy Dampier; NEW YORK, Kristen Kelch (Chief), Ron Arias, Maria Eftimiades, Nancy Matsumoto; WASHINGTON, Garry Clifford (Chief), Linda Kramer, Margie Bonnett Sellinger, Sarah Skolnik, Vornida Seng, Angela Waters
EUROPEAN BUREAU Fred Hauptfuhrer (Chief), Terry Smith (Deputy), Lydia Denworth
SPECIAL CORRESPONDENTS ALBUQUERQUE, Michael Haederle; ATLANTA, Gail Wescott; BALTIMORE, Tom Nugent; BOSTON, S. Avery Brown, Anne Longley; CHICAGO, Bonnie Bell, Leah Eskin, Barbara Sandler, Judy Valente, Fannie Weinstein; DENVER, Vickie Bane; LONDON, Margaret Wright; LOS ANGELES, Leah Feldon-Mitchell, Mitchell Fink, John Griffiths, Carolyn Ramsey, Joyce Wagner; MEMPHIS/NASHVILLE, Jane Sanderson; MIAMI, Don Sider; MINNEAPOLIS, Margaret Nelson; MONACO, Joel Stratte-McClure; PARIS, Cathy Nolan; SAN ANTONIO, Joseph Harmes; TEL AVIV, Mira Avrech; WASHINGTON, Jane Sims Podesta
CONTRIBUTING PHOTOGRAPHERS Marianne Barcellona, Harry Benson, Ian Cook, Tony Costa, Mimi Cotter, Stephen Ellison, Evelyn Floret, Acey Harper, Steve Kagan, Christopher Little, Jim McHugh, Robin Platzer, Neal Preston, Co Rentmeester, Steve Schapiro, Mark Sennet, Peter Serling, Barry Staver, Stanley Tretick, Dale Wittner, Taro Yamasaki
TIME INC. EDITORIAL SERVICES Sheldon Czapnik (Director), Claude Boral (General Manager); Thomas E. Hubbard (Photo Lab); Lany Walden McDonald (Library), Beth Bencini Zarcone (Picture Collection); Thomas Smith (Technology)
TIME INC. EDITORIAL TECHNOLOGY Paul Zazzera (Vice President); Dennis Chesnel
PRESIDENT Ann S. Moore
VICE PRESIDENT Jeremy B. Koch
CIRCULATION DIRECTOR Greg Harris
BUSINESS MANAGER Robert D. Jurgrau
PRODUCTION DIRECTOR Tracy T. Windrum

PUBLISHER Nora P. McAniff
ADVERTISING DEVELOPMENT DIRECTOR William Eydt
ASSISTANT ADVERTISING SALES DIRECTOR John J. Gallagher
MARKETING DIRECTOR Vanessa Reed
EDITORIAL PROJECTS MANAGER Louise Lague

CONTENTS

1995:

Fame Was a Tough Job— But Somebody Had to Do It

To compete with the O.J. trial, *Days of Our Lives* staged an exorcism. The Dancing Itos (right) put *Tonight* back in step. Hugh Grant joined the human comedy with his arrest for…let's call it double parking. With daughter Chelsea, Hillary Cinton played plenipotentiary to Pakistan, where her hair-in-progress remained under wraps.

A READOUT

Think you want to be famous? Sometimes it's not as much fun as it looks. (Sometimes it is, of course, though that's another story.) But just imagine the hassle of being Hugh Grant in 1995. One minute you're a poster boy. The next, you're practically a most-wanted poster. Okay, it was just a mug shot. Even so, it wasn't the kind of publicity still that the Next-Big-Thing in Movies was used to.

Or consider Hillary Clinton. No matter what else she accomplished in 1995, her shifting hairstyles continued to get as much attention as anything important she did. What does it tell you when the First Lady's hair is Washington's most prominent public-works project? Simple: Fame is not for the fainthearted. It takes patience and a willingness to accept that even the small stuff will loom large sometimes.

To the extent that the media contribute to such intense scrutiny and insecurity, we did find ourselves

Public Affairs: More public than ever

increasingly sympathetic to public figures during the year, especially to the more courageous among them. We felt, particularly, for Shannon Faulkner trying to breach the all-male Citadel. Effort counts, and, on a much lesser pop-culture matter, we admired the desperate ingenuity of daytime soap operas to retain viewers when the O.J. trial was already providing the maximum daily dosage of melodrama. And, in terms of food energy alone, can you imagine the drain of being Antonio Banderas, what with four movie releases in 1995 and Melanie Griffith?

Pulling off projects like that with grace is not easy. This is why we think the happiest approach to public life is not to be in it yourself. If the press can be a pain for celebs, it's a comfort and convenience for those in the audience with their nose pressed to the fishbowl. Better just to read about what's going on— up close to all that tumultuous action but not close enough to get bruised. Take Roseanne. Being her, or even just being around her a lot, takes guts. How much better, then, to reflect on her latest doings in the safety of your home, where she can entertain you

but can't fire you or divorce you or otherwise jeopardize your self-esteem?

Let it be said, however, that not every year is so remarkable it deserves its own souvenir yearbook. Whole centuries of the Dark Ages went by without so much as a commemorative T-shirt. But having looked over 1995 with a critic's eye, we've declared it a keepsake year, certainly a lot more deserving of shelf space in your personal library than another volume of cat cartoons. What put '95 over the top for us were what we consider the four essential characteristics of a year for the books.

At the Rock Hall of Fame inaugural in Cleveland, Little Richard backed up a jubilant Yoko Ono. In L.A., Antonio Banderas played *besame mucho* with Melanie Griffith.

One: The O.J. trial. Every year should have one. (Indeed, there were times in 1995 when it seemed that every year *would* have one—the same one— forevermore.)

Two: A walloping public embarrassment. On this score we had concerns for a while. After years of reliable public capering, the British royal family spent the

better part of 1995 decorously hunkered down. But just as we were about to despair, destiny found a parking spot for...Hugh Grant. (This must be what people mean when they say there will always be an England.) And then the Windsors came through, after all, when Princess Diana offered her televised confession of infidelity. The year went out with a bang. And we won't even mention David Letterman on the Oscars.

With his iron-man record (13 years and running), Cal Ripken Jr., worked hard to be a good example; Courtney Love, with Amanda de Cadenet, worked hard to be a bad one. Jim Carrey (with Lauren Holly) got in his licks putting his prints into hallowed cement at Mann's Chinese Theater in L.A.

Three: Another public embarrassment. Okay, we can't help ourselves—David Letterman on the Oscars.

Four: A few examples of uplifting human behavior to help us keep Requirements One to Three in perspective. Which may be why God invented Cal Ripken Jr.

There are other things to be said for 1995. Jennifer Aniston. Babyface. Shania Twain. The gallant example of Christopher Reeve. The computer animation in *Toy Story*. Sandra Bullock in anything. Jim Carrey in everything (or did it just seem that way?). The opening of the Rock and Roll Hall of Fame. And all those other activities we're sure were more fun to read about than to live through. The Lollapalooza tour with Courtney Love. The hullabaloo over Kevin Costner's *Waterworld*. The marital endgame of Cindy Crawford and Richard Gere.

There are other advantages to reading. If only by organizing the headlong confusion of life into chapters, books help us think through our societal pickle. After the year of political posturing on the budget, the disturbing reminders of our racial divide, the troubled Women's Conference in Beijing and the terrorism in Oklahoma City, help was very much in order.

And one final plus of reading: It uses your time economically. A few short-lived events notwithstanding—Connie Chung's anchoring stint, Pete Wilson's presidential campaign, Christie Brinkley's second marriage—most of the things in life take forever to actually do. In reading you cut through the dull stretches to the good parts. In fact, brevity was a lesson we took away from another of the public disclosures that made 1995 so memorable, the diaries of Senator Robert Packwood. They were fascinating in small doses but way too long. We marvel at his impulse to go on so about romance and shopping and personal hair care. A verbatim quote from March 20, 1992: "I just blew my hair. I didn't use any gel on it at all. I just blew it until it was about dry, combed it. . . .It had just the right amount of bounce and wave to it. I came back rather confident."

Even Hillary could empathize with the ostracized Senator on that one.

Public Figures: Sublime to outrageous

Reasonable Doubt: Two icons divide a troubled nation

All America stopped at this moment of decision, when O.J. Simpson was acquitted after his mesmerizing 8½-month murder trial. Meanwhile, Norma McCorvey, the "Jane Roe" of the 1973 Roe v. Wade abortion case, quit her job at a Dallas family-planning clinic and was baptized by antiabortionist Flip Benham, head of Operation Rescue. Though she still accepts legal abortions in the first trimester, McCorvey, 47, said, "I think I've always been pro-life. I just didn't know it."

Pride and Atonement: The Million Man March

Calling for black male solidarity, Nation of Islam leader Louis Farrakhan mobilized a rally of 800,000 plus. Although critics faulted its sexist and separatist overtones and Farrakhan's anti-Semitism, the gathering was clearly a tonic for the soul of its participants.

Reconciliation: Some old foes try to make their peace

Former Alabama governor and reformed segregationist George Wallace, who sent state police against a group of Selma-to-Montgomery civil rights marchers organized by the Rev. Joseph Lowery in 1965, held hands with his ex-nemesis on the 30th anniversary of the event. (Said Lowery: "We both serve a God who can make the desert bloom.") Also seeking a handhold on peace: PLO chief Yasser Arafat, who came to Israel for the first time in three decades to console slain Prime Minister Yitzhak Rabin's widow, Leah; and three Balkan heads of state—(from left) Serb leader Slobodan Milosevic, Bosnian Alija Izetbegovic and Croatian Franjo Tudjam—who initialed an agreement in Dayton, Ohio, after 44 months of savage ethnic war.

Washington Politics: Battling over the budget—and a spot on the '96 ballot

House Speaker Newt Gingrich took the political spotlight—and much of its heat—during the year as he led the GOP attack on big government, big spending and the Big Democrat in the White House. Among those hoping to replace Bill Clinton were Bob Dole, who scoffed at concerns about his age (72) by scuttling through a few laps on his office treadmill, and Phil Gramm and Pat Buchanan, who butted heads for their party's right-wing vote. In May a former conservative hero, Spiro Agnew, 76, returned to town with wife Judy 20 years after leaving the Vice Presidency in disgrace and took his place once again in the Capitol corridors of power—this time as a marble bust.

Photo-Op '95: It's eerie whom they got to juxtapose

(Clockwise, from lower left) Pope John Paul II lent an ear to the animal-rights concerns of Brigitte Bardot, perhaps forgetting that the Vatican condemned her 1956 film *And God Created Woman*. On an Audrey Hepburn-esque call for UNICEF, Julia Roberts was dubbed a "Hollywood Haitian" by President Jean-Bertrand Aristide. Chastity Bono (in jacket) and Candace Gingrich found something in common at a Dallas rally for gays: One is daughter of a California congressman, the other the sister of his boss, the Speaker. At a press fete in D.C., Health and Human Services Secretary Donna Shalala professed to want the autograph of Simpson Trial supporting player Kato Kaelin. And the Duchess of York's jaw dropped, as did the pants of Ivana Trump's man Riccardo Mazzucchelli, when a bingo emcee at Fergie's charity ball for kids ordered the gents: "Trousers down."

A RELUCTANT WARRIOR

Until his graceful retreat from presidential politics, **COLIN POWELL** *led the parade of newsmakers of 1995*

For months, he had seemed ready to turn a page of American political history. Pondering a run for the White House, Colin Powell loomed not merely as the first black presidential candidate to be a viable contender but also perhaps the front-runner. The long slog of the campaign was the one challenge that Powell himself saw as problematic. "You've really got to want it," he said. "You've got to have the fire to do it." Ultimately he concluded that the sparks he had generated around the country during a book-signing tour for his mega-selling memoir, *My American Journey,* had failed to set his own soul afire. When he announced he would not be a candidate, there was much speculation in the press that his wife, Alma (right), had gently dissuaded him from running, partly out of concern for his safety and their privacy. But observers say that the retired Army general never directly asked his wife for a yea or nay vote. "It wasn't all family," says Powell. "I didn't think it was the right thing for me to do at this time."

That display of caution and downright human normalcy seemed only to endear him more to voters. No sooner was he out of the race than pundits noted that at 58, Powell would still be well-placed for a run in the year 2000. For now he will have to be content with giving speeches (at roughly $60,000 a pop). In later appearances he took to reminding listeners that a British journalist reported that he, the Harlem-born son of Jamaican immigrants, was somehow related to Queen Elizabeth II (don't ask). Pausing to let the laughter die, he then cracked, "Forget the presidency, I want to be King!"

"This is a man who has the gift of being himself," friend William Bennett says of Powell (at the new Colin L. Powell Elementary School in The Woodlands, Texas).

Asked if he'd ever run for office, Kennedy said, "I have a few years to make that decision."

JOHN F. KENNEDY JR.

He has carved out a reputation as a sportsman, a flirt, a dilettante—a guy adored by the masses for no reason beyond his pecs and his pedigree. But 1995 was the year that John F. Kennedy Jr. tried to find himself. "It has been an important year," says Onassis biographer C. David Heymann. "Jackie's death liberated him."

So what to do with his freedom? Surprisingly, the long-guarded Kennedy chose a career that would require sacrificing some of his privacy. In September editor-in-chief Kennedy introduced *George,* his glossy new politics-and-pop-culture magazine named for the first Pres. That same month he charmed TV viewers with a cameo appearance on *Murphy Brown.* He even showed up at a July party in New York's Hamptons cuddling and kissing with his favorite date—and rumored fiancée—Carolyn Bessette, a Calvin Klein publicist.

Was all this public display a precursor to a more precarious leap? Kennedy tantalized the curious in an April speech to Detroit executives, saying, "I hope eventually to end up as President . . . [long pause] . . . of a very successful publishing venture." Easier said than done. Though the first issue of *George* sold out its 500,000 copies, the *Rolling Stone-New Republic* hybrid met skepticism from some political professionals who found it lacking in substance. (One feature had Madonna explaining what she would do as President: "The entire armed forces would come out of the closet.") "We pretty quickly decided it wasn't an important player," observed D.C. media critic Stephen Hess. "In serious Washington, it wasn't serious." While having his own magazine is evidence that Kennedy has found some focus in his life, just how serious he is personally remains to be seen. "I have not offered folks a lot about myself, so people traffic in the stuff that they know about," he recently told Dan Rather. "And that's kind of fun."

FRIENDS

Unlike *ER*, the other TV breakthrough hit of the last season, *Friends* never caused viewers to worry that someone's chest was going to be opened with a scalpel. Instead the sitcom about six mildly neurotic twenty-somethings clicked because of the esprit de corps of its offbeat cast (clockwise from upper right: David Schwimmer, Matthew Perry, Matt Le Blanc, Lisa Kudrow, Courteney Cox and Jennifer Aniston). Someday, Cox says, they may develop big egos and big rivalries, and "we'll all go to our big trailers and never speak." Or perhaps Aniston will spill all to *Hard Copy* about Schwimmer's wild nights out with Marcel the monkey. But not yet. Says Perry: "Everyone is open to everyone else's ideas. The deal here is, the funniest joke wins, no matter what." Spoken like a true *Friend*.

ALICIA SILVERSTONE

Alicia Silverstone, the star of the hit movie *Clueless*, is anything but. The savvy 18-year-old, who first found fame as an Aerosmith video vixen, became the darling of the MTV generation for her role as a demented Lolita in the 1993 thriller *The Crush*. In *Clueless*, she portrayed a spoiled Beverly Hills teen who picks her clothes by computer and dismisses admirers with the retort, "As *if!*" But though she herself attended Beverly Hills High, Silverstone is a substantial person who read *Wuthering Heights* between *Clueless* takes and worked with a Shakespeare training company last summer. That doesn't mean she's through with movies: Columbia has signed her to a $10 million, two-picture deal.

BABYFACE

At age 37, Kenneth Edmonds seems to be still growing into his stage name. "The funny thing is, I've gotten more youthful-looking as I've gotten older," says Babyface, whose devotion-filled ballads hearken back to the work of Sam Cooke and the young Smokey Robinson. In a year in which two songs he penned hit No. 1—"I'll Make Love to You" by Boyz II Men and Madonna's "Take a Bow"—and he earned two Grammys, the R & B maestro proved he can still drive women wild. "God," says Madonna, "was in a good mood when he made Babyface."

GREG LOUGANIS

Less than a year after publicly acknowledging that he is gay, Olympic diving champion Greg Louganis revealed in his memoir, *Breaking the Surface*, that he has AIDS and had been abused by his lover, who died of the disease in 1990. Louganis, 35, tested HIV-positive five months before the 1988 Olympic Games in Seoul, where he gashed his head on a diving board during prelims. "I want people to know who I am and what I went through," he wrote. "Then, if parents want their kids to grow up to be like me, I won't have to wonder, 'What if they really knew?'"

ROBERT McNAMARA

Twenty years after the fall of Saigon, former Secretary of Defense Robert McNamara, 78, admitted in a top-selling and controversial new memoir, *In Retrospect*, that he had concluded as early as 1967 that the Vietnam War was unwinnable and that the policies he had helped design to prosecute it were "wrong, terribly wrong." McNamara said it would have given "aid and comfort to the enemy" for him to have spoken out earlier. But former hawks and doves alike were infuriated by McNamara's belated mea culpa. "The real crime is the crime of silence," said David Halberstam, whose 1969 best-seller *The Best and the Brightest* pilloried the architects of the U.S. policies in Vietnam. "It would take a team of psychiatrists to understand Robert McNamara. He's the most divided man in public life I've ever seen."

MICHAEL CRICHTON

Even if he weren't 6'9", Michael Crichton, 53, towers over the pop culture. He was the executive producer of TV's hottest show, *ER*, and followed *Jurassic Park*—the basis for the most successful movie in history—with a sequel, *The Lost World*, expected to sell 2 million hardcover alone. His estimated '95 earnings (including the film version of *Congo*): $22 million.

ELLEN DeGeneres

A self-aware goofiness made Ellen DeGeneres, 37, the Funny Girl of 1995. Her sassy sitcom, *Ellen*, consistently won its time slot and her book, *My Point...and I Do Have One*, topped the best-seller list. During *Ellen*'s spring hiatus, she was busy shooting her movie debut, *Mr. Wrong*, a dark comedy about a good date gone sour. "I hear it came down to me and Sharon Stone," she said. "Actually most parts come down to me and Sharon Stone. Originally they were going to call my show *Sharon*."

KEITH LOCKHART

Keith Lockhart, 35, who in 1995 became only the third conductor of the Boston Pops orchestra in the last 65 years, likes some pizzazz in the concert hall. In his previous job with the Cincinnati Symphony he once Rollerbladed onto the stage. Other times he was suspended from a guy wire or jumped out of a giant birthday cake. "I'm a populist musician," he says. "Music is entertainment whether it's cutting edge or 300 years old."

RAND & ROBYN MILLER

The Miller brothers—Rand, 35, (standing) and Robyn, 28—are the brains behind *Myst*, an eerily beautiful CD-ROM adventure set on a deserted island. Having sold more than 500,000 copies of the original *Myst* since 1993, the Millers are at work on a sequel and have a $1 million contract with Hyperion, a publishing subsidiary of Disney, for the rights to three future *Myst* novels. So what makes *Myst* so seductive? "Time doesn't matter," says Rand, who himself needs two hours to navigate all of the *Myst*y dimensions. "*Myst* is just an excuse for an adult to get lost in another world for a while."

THE PIG & THE POC

Pocahontas, the Indian princess who befriended English settlers in the Chesapeake Bay region in the early 1600s, returned as a buxom Disney cartoon beauty in 1995 and found herself competing for the affection of young moviegoers with an anthropomorphic porker. *Pocahontas* grossed more than $140 million, but *Babe*, a surprise charmer, brought home some $53 million of bacon.

ANTONIO BANDERAS

The Valentino of 1995, Antonio Banderas kept fans panting as he bounded from one movie to the next. He had killer roles as a hitman in *Assassins* and a guy out to avenge his dead wife in *Desperado*. He played a mystery man who gave Rebecca De Mornay sexual thrills and chills in *Never Talk to Strangers*. Then turning to comedy in *Too Much*, due out this winter, he portrayed a man so desperate for the affections of Daryl Hannah and Melanie Griffith that he pretended to be twins. Offscreen he and Griffith made no secret of their hots for each other. Splitting with his wife of eight years, actress Ana Leza, Banderas kept Griffith company while she filmed *Lolita*. If he can find time, Banderas hopes to return to his native Spain someday to direct *Don Juan*. For now, he is happy, at 35, to play the role in real life.

HOOTIE & THE BLOWFISH

Forget Buttafuoco, Gillooly and Boutros Boutros-Ghali. A favorite running gag for David Letterman in '95 was "Hootie and the Blowfish." With a boost from Dave, the once obscure South Carolina bar band (from top: Dean Felber, 27, Jim Sonefeld, 30, Darius Rucker, 28, Mark Bryan, 27) sold more than 5 million copies of their debut album, *Cracked Rear View*. But the self-styled dweebs of rock insist the Blowfish are still regular guys and no blowhards. "I mean, we used to eat Mrs. Paul's frozen fish sticks," says Sonefeld. "Now we eat these little chilled shrimp. Same thing."

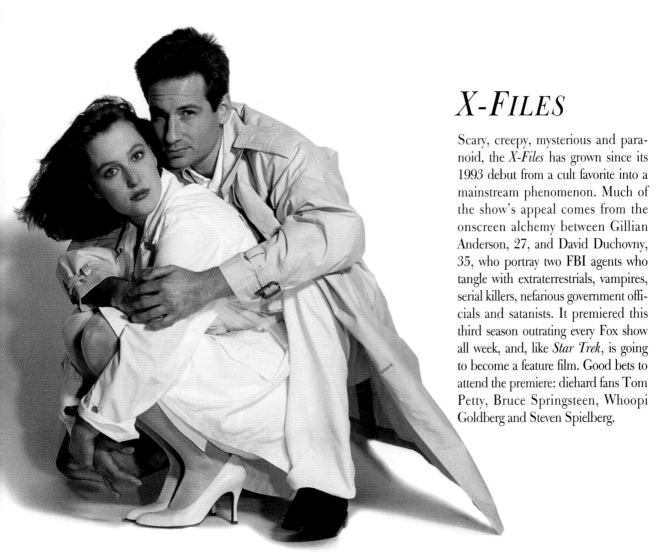

X-FILES

Scary, creepy, mysterious and paranoid, the *X-Files* has grown since its 1993 debut from a cult favorite into a mainstream phenomenon. Much of the show's appeal comes from the onscreen alchemy between Gillian Anderson, 27, and David Duchovny, 35, who portray two FBI agents who tangle with extraterrestrials, vampires, serial killers, nefarious government officials and satanists. It premiered this third season outrating every Fox show all week, and, like *Star Trek*, is going to become a feature film. Good bets to attend the premiere: diehard fans Tom Petty, Bruce Springsteen, Whoopi Goldberg and Steven Spielberg.

SHANIA TWAIN

Country's newest star, Shania Twain, 29, is definitely living up to her name, which means "on her way" in Ojibway. Her second album, *The Woman in Me*, and the single "Any Man of Mine" both hit No. 1 on the country charts, and "Whose Bed Have Your Boots Been Under?" is a title for the ages. After growing up in such poverty in Ontario that she often went to school without lunch, Twain now lives on a 20-square-mile estate in Upstate New York with music producer Robert John "Mutt" Lange, whom she wed a year ago. An aching lullaby on her album, "God Bless the Child," was written after her parents died in a car accident seven years ago. "I felt totally lost," she says, "and that song was my crying out. I sang it until I met Mutt." Now, she says, "I don't feel lost anymore."

GRANT HILL

In an era of in-your-face stars, Grant Hill is more than a superjock—he is intelligent and genuinely civil. As pro basketball's Air (Jordan) apparent, the 6'8", 225-lb. Detroit Piston rose to NBA stardom so quickly it nearly gave his agent whiplash. Yet even with an eight-year, $45 million contract, a standout rookie season and his own sneaker ("The Hill"), the 22-year-old sports an undersized ego. "I have a slight case of love handles, and my hair grows so fast, people call me Chia Pet," concedes Hill. "I'd like to think that my personality is what people find attractive."

RALPH REED

After helping get out the vote for the Republican landslide a year ago, Ralph Reed, 33, and his Christian Coalition anted up $1 million to support the Contract with America, and he published his own manifesto, *Politically Incorrect*. A rowdy at the University of Georgia, Reed became a teetotaler in 1983 and the next year met his wife-to-be, a Jesse Helms campaign worker. "Our group is blessed with having a large megaphone," he says of his 1.5 million members, "and we can set the tone for the country."

JAMES FINN GARNER

Who knew that Hans Christian Andersen needed sensitivity training? Or that the Brothers Grimm were sexist and classist? Sad but true, according to James Finn Garner, 34, who followed his 1994 super-seller, *Politically Correct Bedtime Stories*, with two more best-list volumes of sanitized, satirical fairy tales: *Once Upon a More Enlightened Time* and *Politically Correct Holiday Stories*. Nothing is sacred in Garner's skewed prism: Even the tortoise who outran the hare is disqualified after urinalysis shows him to be "a heavy user and abuser of steroids."

STEVEN COVEY

The maxims Steven R. Covey, 63, set forth in *Seven Habits of Highly Effective People* in 1989—"Begin with the End in Mind" is Habit 2—are as easy to digest as Forrest Gump's box of chocolates, but simplicity sells, and, at recent count, had moved 5 million copies. In '95, they became part of Microsoft's time-management software and earned new fans in lofty places. House Speaker Newt Gingrich calls *Seven Habits* a "must read," and President Clinton powwowed with the self-help savant at Camp David. But Covey, a Utah Republican, insists he doesn't play political favorites professionally: "We're Americans first. These principles are universal."

DEAN ORNISH

For heart disease, Dr. Dean Ornish, 41, prescribes the familiar old tough medicine—a virtually fat-free diet and exercise—plus getting in touch with your feelings. But his books, *Dr. Dean Ornish's Program for Reversing Heart Disease* (1990) and *Eat More, Weigh Less* (1993), have become best-sellers and attracted a celeb following including Ted Danson, Bill Moyers and Marlon Brando. Now the doc is approaching guruhood as another chubster, Bill Clinton, signed on, and Hillary asked him to rework the White House menu.

MARC ANDREESSEN

Two years ago, Marc Andreessen earned $6.85 an hour at a university computer lab. Today the 24-year-old software developer is worth more than $50 million after a public stock offering by his company, Netscape Communications—creators of the Navigator program that most Internet junkies use to browse the World Wide Web. "He's not a typical computer nerd," says his girlfriend, Elizabeth Horn. "He's well-dressed. And he bathes a lot."

SANDRA BULLOCK

What a difference one summer makes. Before her role in 1994's *Speed* made her America's most bussable star, Sandra Bullock, 31, was languishing in second-tier roles in movies like *Demolition Man* and nursing a bruised heart after the breakup of a three-year relationship with actor Tate Donovan. In 1995, she won raves in *While You Were Sleeping*, raked in $6 million for her role as a hacker in *The Net*, and was seen with Dallas Cowboys quarterback Troy Aikman. What caused the sudden Bullock boom? *Net* director Irwin Winkler has a theory. "Sandra doesn't have a star attitude," he says. "People see a lot of themselves in her."

COMEBACKS & RECOVERIES

In the simpler times chronicled by William Shakespeare, all the world was a stage. In today's more troublous, 12-step era, it's all a recovery room. In 1995, many who strutted and fretted their hour across the American landscape struggled valiantly to overcome accidents, illness, tragedy, fear and, in some cases, infamy.

More than two years after she was knifed by a crazed fan of her rival Steffi Graf, Monica Seles, 21, made a smashing return to the tennis tour. "I had to deal with emotions I didn't even know existed in my mind," she conceded. Violin prodigy Rachel Barton, 20, overcame the loss of a leg in a freak train accident to dazzle audiences in Chicago (above left). Even Pee-wee Herman's alter ego, Paul Reubens, 42, who four years ago was busted for overexposure in a Florida porn theater, popped up again on Murphy Brown *(right) and in a featured role in the movie comedy* Matilda.

As the ruthless Dallas oilman J.R. Ewing, he was shot in front of 83 million viewers and then came back; in 1995, Larry Hagman, 64, and another reformed alcoholic—singer David Crosby—both received life saving liver transplants. Putting her bulimia and a broken marriage to actor Emilio Estevez behind her, Paula Abdul, 32, sang a brave new song with the release of her third album, Head Over Heels. And after three years in prison for rape, Mike Tyson, 29, emerged with a new woman in his corner—med school grad Monica Turner—and sent his shock-coiffed manager, Don King, into ecstasy when he kayoed Peter "Hurricane" McNeeley in 89 seconds.

TRIALS & TRIBULATIONS

THE GLOVE DIDN'T FIT

went free in a year when Susan Smith got life and a talk show caused a death

It ended as it began. Less than 17 months before, a nation watched in shock as O.J. Simpson and his old football teammate Al Cowlings took their eerie freeway ride in a white Bronco. How could this affable sports hero, product-pitcher and occasional movie actor have butchered his ex-wife Nicole and her friend Ron Goldman? After a 474-day legal pageant that was alternately tedious, farcical and lurid, many were even more stunned when air-borne cameras again followed Simpson in a white vehicle: This time he was making a triumphal return to his Rockingham estate. TV cameras showed black law students at Howard University cheering when they heard of the acquittal. But outside the courthouse, women protested the verdict with signs reading "Wife Beaters Are Not Heroes." Social commenta-

Amid the drama of the trial, the blood-soaked murder gloves were too tight, and Judge Lance Ito, 45 (here examining DNA evidence), was too loose in controlling attorneys' antics.

tors dissected the case as a gauge of our seemingly irreversible racial divisions, of the flaws of our police forces and the criminal justice system, and of the relentless tabloiding of America. But what of the impact on lives that were changed forever by the crime and the trial—the anguished families, the jurors, the attorneys, the witnesses as well as the defendant and the two children he had with Nicole? As one friend put it: "No one who had anything to do with O.J. and Nicole will ever be the same."

Those close to Nicole who saw the yellowing bruises and raw abrasions of spousal abuse years before her death were convinced that Simpson was guilty. She "had a strong backbone," says friend Eve Chen, bemoaning her own helplessness and Nicole's shunning of counseling. "She didn't want to bring out her troubles." "If Nicole had [been told] time after time, 'You don't need to take this. . . .' " says another friend, "maybe it would have saved her life."

Simpson, 48, who spent more than $6 million on his defense, faces the Lizzie Borden dilemma: He was cleared of murder, but many still think he's guilty. For a man who bloomed in the limelight, his anguish in the shadows is apparent. He finds himself jeered and unwelcome at the golf clubs where he once lived on lionization. He reluctantly canceled an NBC *Dateline* appearance on the advice of lawyer Johnnie Cochran, but called *The New York Times* to deliver a wandering exculpation of his character. His days of endorsing products like Hertz (for $550,000 per year) are over, his movie career in the can. Simpson's girlfriend, model Paula Barbieri, ended their affair publicly on ABC's *Primetime Live*, complaining that their Florida reunion was a sham to provide Simpson a lucrative photo shoot for the tabloid *Star*.

But how will O.J. support his lifestyle and his son Justin, 7, and

Darden (above), the moral force of the trial, never let the jury forget that Nicole was slashed so ferociously in the throat that she was almost decapitated. A game and beleaguered Clark (below) tried to stack the logistics against O.J. and to cut through what she derided as defense "smoke screens."

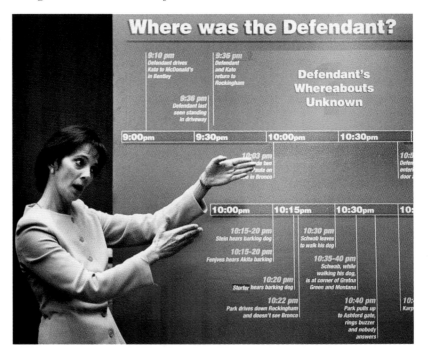

daughter Sydney, 9, his two children with Nicole? During his imprisonment, the young children lived with their maternal grandparents, the Browns. After his release, O.J. vowed in a statement that his children would be "raised the way that Nicole and I had always planned." The Browns, says an insider, will not oppose the return of the children to their father.

For funds, Simpson may have to sell his $2.9 million Brentwood mansion. "It's the most famous house in the world," says L.A. Realtor Elaine Young. "Like Graceland. Maybe bigger." Come spring, Simpson is scheduled to be tried for wrongful death on civil charges brought by the victims' families, who are asking unspecified damages. "It doesn't have anything to do with money," says Ron's sister, Kim Goldman. "If we can make him [Simpson] feel a quarter of the pain we feel, it's worth it."

Lawyers from the prosecution were putting their own lives back together, helped by cushy publishing deals. Lead prosecutor Marcia Clark would get $4.2 million. All nerve and outrage, Clark, 41, became a working-woman role model, clearly torn between home and career. Her estranged husband pressed in their divorce case for sole custody of the couple's two children, claiming Clark was too busy with the trial to offer proper care. Her disillusioned colleague Christopher Darden, 38, whose literary payoff was $1.3 million, was so sour after the verdict he said he would take a year off from the law. The two district attorneys have similar temperaments—spontaneous and passionate—and spent so much of their 14-hour days together that they relate, says one colleague, "like brother and sister." Or would it be man and wife? the press speculated, after they were seen together post-trial.

Across the aisle, the Dream Team ended up becoming one another's worst nightmare. Although they suc-

The defense charged that the L.A.P.D.'s Mark Furhrman, 43, who repeatedly used the "N" word on tape, planted evidence. Shapiro said he was "appalled" by colleague Cochran's "hat trick" and "playing the race card . . . from the bottom of the deck." Below, O.J. confers with his unsung star consultant, Jo-Ellan Dimitrius, who vetted the original jury choices and held mock-jury focus groups to fine-tune the defense approach.

At the emotional end of what resembled, finally, a B-movie verité, Simpson exulted at the verdict, flanked by his Dream Team members F. Lee Bailey (above, left) and Cochran. The family, including O.J.'s mother, Eunice (below, left), daughter Arnelle, first wife Marguerite, son Jason and sister Shirley Baker wept tears of joy. Afterward, Jason read a statement of his father's vowing to track down the real murderer and offering a reward for information.

cessfully raised "reasonable doubt" in the minds of jurors (in part by stressing the L.A.P.D.'s ineptness and racism), original chief defense lawyer Robert Shapiro, 53, seethed when he was shouldered aside by the showboating and mesmerizing Johnnie L. Cochran Jr., 58. F. Lee Bailey, 62, meanwhile, was intent on rejuvenating his flagging career. "I thought I would be leading a team of professionals," said Shapiro. "I was wrong." Cochran's publishing advance was reportedly $2.5 million, Shapiro's $1.5 million. The team's skilled DNA specialist, Barry Scheck, took heat from the Jewish community in New York City when Cochran drew moral parallels between Simpson and the victims of Nazism. Criticism from groups opposing domestic violence particularly hurt Scheck, who represented the abused Hedda Nussbaum in her 1988 trial. "I am tired of being on television," said Scheck. "I am tired of this whole thing."

Equally exhausted and disoriented were the trial's most important supporting players: the 12 citizens of the sequestered jury and two alternates who sat through the numbing expert testimony and the capricious sidebars. (Ten jurors were dismissed during the course of the trial, their places taken by alternates.) Finally, said computer technician Brenda Moran, known to the world only as juror No. 7 until the surprising verdict was reached in just four hours: "I feel free. If another jury summons comes in," she mused, "I'm gonna tear it up." So might we all.

When the decision was read, Ron Goldman's sister, Kim (above), collapsed in the arms of her father, Fred. Visiting Nicole's grave: parents Louis and Juditha Brown (standing with dog, Kato), sister Dominque Brown (seated at left) holding her son Aaron and O.J.'s daughter Sydney, sister Tanya Brown with O.J.'s son Justin and sister Denise with her son Sean.

HOW COULD HUGH?

Hugh Grant, the shy, beguiling Brit who shot to stardom as the bumbling bachelor in 1994's surprise smash *Four Weddings and a Funeral*, was once every mother's dream: a clever and charming lad who loved his mum and dad, adored his long-time girlfriend (29-year-old Estée Lauder model Elizabeth Hurley), was bold enough to be naughty ("I've always had a crush on cheerleaders—Catholic cheerleaders—my double favorite," he recently quipped), modest enough to be embarrassed by the fuss of fame ("The money offers are hysterical. They make me giggle," he said) and yet honest enough to admit that, well, yes, he was quite fond of the attention and other rewards that fame brings.

Then Grant, 34, went up a Hollywood street and came down on the wrong side of the vice squad. In L.A. to promote *Nine Months*, a comedy about a man who flips—and not with delight—when he learns his girlfriend is pregnant, Grant pulled his white BMW to a street curb around 1:30 a.m. on June 27 and exchanged words with Divine Marie Brown, 23, a prostitute. Brown climbed into Grant's car, and a few minutes later two policemen arrested the pair for engaging in oral sex. Within hours, media the world over were trumpeting the news, and the man who until then had never met a situation he couldn't finesse with a glib felicity issued a seemingly heartfelt statement. "Last night I did something completely insane," Grant said. "I have hurt people I love and embarrassed people I work with. For both things I am more sorry than I can ever possibly say."

Grant subsequently pleaded no contest to a charge of lewd conduct in a public place and was ordered to pay $1,180, serve two years' probation and complete an AIDS education program. Meanwhile, he kept his commitment to publicize *Nine Months*, and fessed up to his tryst in every conceivable kind of cathode confessional: late night (*Tonight*), cable (*Larry King Live*), morning (*The Today Show*) and daytime chat (*Live with Regis & Kathie Lee*).

Even more surprising than Grant's candor was that he showed up at the L.A. premiere for *Nine Months*, with the girlfriend many speculated might dump him. Hurley's expressions ran the gamut from blank to taciturn, and she looked the very embodiment of mixed emotions in her white mini-dress. But a few months later the couple announced plans to coproduce and costar in *Extreme Measures*, a medical thriller.

So what did Grant learn from his embarrassing adventure? "You know in life what's a good thing to do and what's a bad thing," he told Jay Leno on *Tonight*, "I did a bad thing, and there you have it."

Divine Brown (left) pocketed $160,000 from a British tabloid for her tale of the tryst, and Hugh Grant told all to Larry King, but Elizabeth Hurley was tight-lipped when they showed up at the L.A. premiere of Nine Months.

FATAL ATTRACTION

For Scott Amedure, 32, flying to Chicago to share his romantic fantasies with chat show host Jenny Jones was a thrill. The unemployed gay bartender from Orion Township, Michigan, couldn't get enough of sensation-seeking daytime TV. Jon Schmitz too was excited about appearing on the *Jenny Jones Show*. A waiter in the Detroit suburb of Bloomfield Hills, Schmitz, 24, had been told by producers that he had a secret admirer who would step forward during the taping. A few months earlier Schmitz had split with his fiancée, and he was eager for a new relationship. So before leaving, he spent $300 on new clothes in hopes of impressing his admirer.

Schmitz's dream began to deflate the moment he was ushered in front of a tittering audience that obviously knew something he didn't. Onstage in the studio was Donna Riley, Schmitz's upstairs neighbor. Assum-

ing Donna was the one who was smitten with him, Schmitz gave her a hug. Then, as the audience guffawed, Jones told Schmitz that Amedure, who was seated next to Riley—and whom Schmitz barely knew—was the one nursing a crush. "You have to be flattered," Jones said. Although Schmitz would later tell police that he had felt "almost sick to his stomach," he seemed to react calmly. He said, "Yes, but I'm a heterosexual. I'm not interested." The audience applauded and roared.

Three days later, Amedure lay dead in his kitchen, killed by two shotgun blasts to the chest. Fifteen minutes after the shots were fired, Schmitz dialed 911 and confessed. Charged with murder, he told police that he felt "humiliated" by his *Jenny Jones* experience. As he explained it to the 911 operator, "He [Amedure] f----- me on national TV." In the wake of the tragedy, Oakland County, Michigan, prosecutor Richard Thompson maintained the program's staff "displayed incredible insensitivity and irresponsibility. They seem to follow the rule that anything goes in the pursuit of ratings." But Jenny Jones insisted Schmitz had been warned beforehand that his admirer could be either a man or a woman. "We have no responsibility whatsoever because he was not misled." she said. "This was not an ambush show." In any case, the producers had the good grace not to air the episode.

"It was a tragedy that shouldn't have happened," said Jenny Jones after Jon Schmitz (below) shot Scott Amedure (above).

Some critics questioned whether Shannon Faulkner reported in too heavy for the boot-camp regimen at the Citadel.

HER WAR IS OVER

It had seemed a modest enough ambition in modern America: to be the first female cadet at the Citadel, the Charleston, South Carolina, military college whose students, 134 years ago, fired the first shots in slavery's defense. But it turned out to be harder than Shannon Faulkner, 20, ever expected. Since 1993, when a federal judge ordered the fiercely traditional college to allow Faulkner to attend day classes, she had been the focus of a war waged in the courts and on the campus, where the boot-camp rigors of the school's Hell Week orientation finally left her dreams in ruins. "In the end it all came down to me," she says. "It's a burden that's too great to put on one person's shoulders."

On the first day of Hell Week, during which freshmen "knobs" are taught military discipline by abusive upperclassmen in 100-degree heat, Faulkner strained to keep a one-of-the-guys front. But a knot began to twist in her stomach and, over lunch—mandatory heaps of Beefaroni—her body rebelled. For the next four days Faulkner stayed mostly in the infirmary, stricken with nausea and heat sickness. "I could hear the guys marching by outside," she says. "I just kept saying, 'I'm going to get back out there.' " But when her nausea failed to subside, she finally surrendered. "I was emotionally wiped out," she says. Though 24 men also threw in the towel, none received the attention accorded Faulkner. "Cadets are told to get in shape before they arrive," says Citadel spokesman Col. Terry Leedom. "She didn't. She learned, along with the guys who couldn't take it, that this isn't a rest home."

After Faulkner returned home to Powdersville, South Carolina, author Pat Conroy, a Citadel grad who has been scathingly critical of the place, arrived with a cooler stuffed with fresh shrimp. And Faulkner insisted she was glad to have at least made a run at the walls of the all-male academy. "I won't ever shy away from admitting that I did this," she says. "I'm proud. Damn proud."

Tears of Rage, Tears of Pity

As the trial drew to a conclusion, Michael and Alex Smith, 3 and 14 months, finally had their day in court. Slowly, their father, David, 25, walked up and down the length of the jury box in the Union, South Carolina, courtroom, letting each juror get a look at snapshots of the two boys. Then he described what his life has been like since his then-estranged wife, Susan, 23, drowned their sons Michael and Alex in John D. Long Lake, as they sat strapped in the back seat of her Mazda. "I don't know what I'm supposed to do without my kids," David said, choking back tears. Later, as Susan passed David on her way out of the courtroom, she let out a soft cry as painful as it was futile. "I'm sorry, David," she said.

Originally, Susan had cynically tried to blame a black carjacker for the disappearance of her boys and acted out that lie for nine days, playing for public sympathy that turned to outrage when she was exposed. But after prosecutor Tommy Pope announced he would seek the death penalty, many folks around Union softened their once-harsh views. That included Shirley McCloud, who lives in the house Smith first ran to the night the boys disappeared. Says McCloud: "There just had to be something terribly wrong with her for this to have happened."

Compassion toward Smith grew as details of her sad and sordid past came to light. Her natural father, Harry Vaughan, a fireman, committed suicide by shooting himself in the head when Susan was 6, and her step-

Susan Smith's husband, David, stood by her at first, but was unmoved by her tears after she finally confessed to drowning their two kids in a lake (right).

father, Beverly Russell, a financial planner and a leader in the state Christian Coalition, admitted that he had molested her as a teenager. Susan herself attempted suicide at least twice, the first at age 13, when she overdosed on over-the-counter drugs. Her mother is uncertain what precipitated the crisis. Susan's marriage in 1991, at age 19, to David Smith didn't help get her back on track. The pair were constantly at odds, and sexually involved with other people. David dated other

employees at the Winn-Dixie super-market where he worked. And while continuing to sleep with David, Susan started seeing Tom Findlay, the wealthiest and most eligible young man in Union. In the weeks before she killed her sons, she frolicked nude in a hot tub with another man at the Findlay mansion.

In the end, of course, Susan's unhappy past could not explain—let alone excuse—the killing of her two boys. But it took the jury just 2½

hours to reject the death penalty and sentence her to life in prison. And the catalog of her traumas offered a cautionary tale of how a family can self-destruct. David acknowledged as much in his book, *Beyond All Reason: My Life With Susan Smith*. "Nothing," he wrote with supreme understatement, "can ever approach the horror of what happened to Michael and Alex, but some of the background leading up to it does not show human behavior at its best."

47

PASSING THE BUCKS

Rep. Enid Waldholtz, 37, of Salt Lake City was one of the new-wave Republican fire-brands who swept into Washington in 1995, promising an end to business as usual on Capitol Hill. A devoted acolyte of House Speaker Newt Gingrich, she became the GOP's family-values poster mom with the birth of her daughter Elizabeth in August, making her only the second U.S. representative to have a child while in office. Now, following the arrest of her husband of two years, Joe Waldholtz, 32, for alleged financial improprieties, she became Exhibit A for the urgency of campaign-expense reform.

With Joe serving as her campaign treasurer, Waldholtz spent more than any other House freshman in the country—$1.8 million—to win her seat. And they lived in a townhouse once owned by Henry Kissinger renting at $3,800 per month. But the precarious house Joe built of borrowed credit cards and bogus accounts collapsed and threatened his wife's future in Congress, where she has become known as the "Mormon Maggie Thatcher" for her fiscal and social conservatism. An FBI investigation uncovered a suspected $1.6 million check-kiting scheme in which Joe allegedly shuffled money between bank accounts to cover up a shortage of funds. Joe allegedly also ran up

$45,000 on a staffer's credit card. And he was ordered by a Pittsburgh court to provide details about his management of $600,000 belonging to his Alzheimer's-stricken grandmother.

Enid filed for divorce, seeking sole custody of Elizabeth. But if investigators discover Enid knew about the financial irregularities, she could face charges too. Meanwhile, a poll taken at the time of Joe's arrest indicated 36 percent of her constituents felt she should resign immediately, and 61 percent thought she shouldn't seek a second term. "Enid could have put a stop to this a long time ago," says Steve Taggart, her campaign press secretary. He resigned in 1994 over concerns about the financial chaos.

"I trusted him. I was wrong," says Enid Waldholtz (with husband Joe, baby Elizabeth and a staffer before Joe's arrest).

An avid sportsman, Christopher Reeve often practiced riding several hours a day before his near-fatal accident. At his first public appearance since being paralyzed, Reeve was greeted by Robin Williams (right). Another of the 500 guests at the gathering, actress Blythe Danner, said, "It's like Christmas having Chris here."

MAN OF STEEL TAKES A FALL

At the spring horse trials of the Commonwealth Dressage and Combined Training Association in Culpeper County, Virginia, actor and riding enthusiast Christopher Reeve, 42, seemed focused as he took Eastern Express, a 7-year-old Thoroughbred, galloping toward a three-foot-high rail jump. "The horse was coming into the fence beautifully," recalls Lisa Reid, 42, a horse trainer. "The rhythm was fine and Chris was fine, and they were going at a good pace." But then, says Reid, that seamless synergy between horse and rider dissolved suddenly. "The horse put his front feet over the fence, but his hind feet never left the ground," she says. "Chris is such a big

man. He was going forward, his head over the top of the horse's head."

The fall caused multiple fractures in Reeve's spinal column and left the film Superman unable to use any of his limbs or even to breathe without the aid of a respirator. But it did not crush his spirit. "Five days after my accident I had a 50-50 chance to live," Reeve told a ballroom full of celebrities just four months later at the annual dinner of the Creative Coalition, an advocacy group for issues ranging from arts funding to health care. "I was hanging upside down [at the hospital] and I looked and saw a blue scrub hat and yellow gown and heard this Russian accent. There was Robin Williams being some insane Russian doctor. I knew I was going to be all right."

Upon arriving for the dinner in an electric wheelchair—to a five-minute standing ovation—Reeve explained why he'd come. One of his former English teachers, he recalled, would not abide students missing class: "He said, 'The only excuse for nonattendance is quadruple amputation,' so I thought I'd better show up." He introduced his wife Dana, 34, who, with their son, Will, 2, had kept a bedside vigil after the accident: "I owe her my life." Then Williams took the stage.

Robin, who has known Reeve since they were drama students at Juilliard 22 years ago, praised his friend's work for the Creative Coalition. "You're on a roll, bro," he said. Then with a twinkle, he glanced at the wheelchair and added, "Literally."

49

SAVIORS & SURVIVORS

COURAGE AND CARING IN THE FACE OF TERROR

In a year for heroes and in the wake of a horrifying bomb attack, **OKLAHOMA CITY** *and the nation united to share the grief*

I n a world torn and tortured by terrorism, Americans hoped and prayed that it wouldn't happen here. But on April 19, 1995, the Alfred P. Murrah Federal Building in Oklahoma City was blown apart in an explosion of nearly unimaginable force. Claiming 169 innocent victims, it was the worst terrorist attack against civilians in U.S. history. When authorities arrested the accused mastermind—former Army sergeant Timothy James McVeigh, 27—he refused to provide more than his name, rank and serial number, declaring that he was a prisoner of war. The implication was clear: He saw himself as a revolutionary now in the hands of a government he hoped to destroy.

As the nation reeled from the bombing, the dramatic image (left) of the lifeless body of 1-year-old Baylee Almon being cradled by firefighter Captain Chris Fields would soon become, in the words of Oklahoma Governor Frank Keating, "a metaphor for what happened here." It was Oklahoma City police sergeant John Avera, 47, who less than half an hour after the explosion of the 4,800-lb. fuel-oil-and-fertilizer device, helped dig Baylee from the ruins of what had been the America's Kids day-care center. "It was dark," he recalls. "We couldn't see the babies, but we could hear them cry." Beneath a chunk of concrete, Avera and a fellow officer found two babies. Grabbing one, Avera recounts how he "ran out of the building with her as fast as I could." He didn't stop until he saw firefighter Fields, 30. "I've got a 'critical,' " he told him, asking for help. "I can't find any signs of life." As Avera passed the child to Fields, Charles H. Porter IV, 25, a banker and amateur photographer who had run to the site from his nearby office, shot the scene from across the street with a zoom lens. Within four hours his pictures, which were developed at a Wal-Mart photo shop, were being distributed worldwide by the Associated Press. The following Sunday, 12,000 mourners filled the Oklahoma State Fairgrounds for a special service. President Bill Clinton and the Rev. Billy Graham presided and told some of the many stories of unspeakable pain and ineffable heroism. Here are four:

REBECCA ANDERSON and her husband, Fred, both 37, were relaxing at home in Midwest City, Oklahoma, when they heard the explosion 30 miles away. After watching a TV report, Rebecca, a licensed practical nurse, rushed into the bedroom and shouted to her husband to get into the car. "She saw some fireman carrying a kid out, or something, and said they could use some help," he recalls. Tragically, Anderson never got to help. Shortly after her husband, a delivery truck driver, dropped her off at the bombing scene, she was apparently hit on the back of the head by falling debris. Although she initially declined medical attention—"She kept insisting she had to get back and help the wounded," says rescue worker Glenn Sheppard—she collapsed minutes later and was rushed to the hospital, where she died four days later from massive swelling in the brain.

AS HE RACED TO THE SITE of the bombing, Dr. Andy Sullivan remembered the axiom he'd heard about medics in Vietnam: The only doctors who got killed were those who were where they didn't belong. "When I crossed the police barrier," says Sullivan, 51, an orthopedic surgeon, "I thought, 'I don't belong here.' " But he also knew he was needed. Firefighters had discovered Dana Bradley, a 20-year-old mother of two, trapped in the building's basement and couldn't move her because a huge concrete beam, which was crushing her right leg just below the knee, was holding up the central portion of the building. Sullivan told Bradley they would have to amputate her right leg and she said, "Do what you have to do." As Sullivan prepared to crawl into the crevice where Bradley lay, he remembers thinking, "I may never see my family again if this falls." Unable to see, Sullivan operated by touch as he severed the muscles, tendons and ligaments surrounding Bradley's knee with the four surgical knives he had brought in an amputation kit. But one by one, the carbon blades became dull. Finally, he reached into his back pocket for his own pocketknife. "It was new and it was sharp," he says. After about 10 minutes the limb was free. Bradley survived, but her mother, Cheryl Hammons, 44, and her children Peachlyn, 3, and Gabrion, 4 months, all of whom had accompanied her to the Social Security office, did not.

WHEN SURGEON RICK NELSON, 38, arrived at the building, he thought he was too late until, he recalls, "Someone came out yelling, 'We've got a live one!' " Deep in the basement, Bronte, a Rottweiler rescue dog, had sniffed out the foot of Brandy Ligons, 15. (In fact, in his excitement, the dog had nipped it.) The teenager, who had been at the Social Security office before the blast, was entombed in a deadly maze of rubble. Nelson knew they were in a race against time. "For the last 20 minutes," he recalls, "she was fading in and out." Nelson administered oxygen and made sure that once out of the debris, Ligons was stable on a backboard for her trip to a hospital, where her spleen was removed and she was treated for pulmonary contusions. "I feel such a sense of sorrow about all this," says Nelson of the victims he couldn't heal. "The fact that we got Brandy out is what I hang on to." Brandy, recovered, is back in school, dreaming of becoming a lawyer, and Dr. Nelson has set up a trust fund to help.

THE MORNING OF THE BOMBING, Melva Noakes, 43, who became a foster parent 25 years before and owned the America's Kids day-care center, was doing the payroll at a sister center in Choctaw, Oklahoma. At 9 a.m. she made a check-in call with Dana Cooper, 24, who ran the federal building center. But soon after Noakes hung up, she felt the shudder of an explosion. "We saw a jet and thought it must have been a sonic boom," says Noakes. She had heard the bomb from 20 miles away. Now she is left with a grief that may never fade. "We've all lost something," Noakes says, speaking for Americans everywhere. "We're all holding each other's hands."

"All the babies I held the day before are gone," says Melva Noakes (placing a wreath at the site). Accused terrorist Timothy McVeigh was a gun-loving militiaman who made a pilgrimage to the Branch Davidian compound in Waco.

The Pres basks in the pilot's unalloyed popularity. Afterward they shared a cigar on the White House balcony.

HERO'S WELCOME

As he stepped out of a C-20 military plane and onto the sun-baked tarmac at Andrews Air Force Base in Washington, D.C., Captain Scott O'Grady, 29, looked pale and wan, having lost 10 pounds off his wiry 5'9" frame. Three days earlier, the Air Force fighter pilot had emerged from a harrowing week in a Bosnian forest, and his fantastic hide-and-seek tale had quickly entered American folklore. After his F-16 was bisected by a Serb missile during a United Nations mission over Bosnia, he had ejected and taken cover for nearly a week in the woods and pastureland, dining on ants, leaves, grass and rainwater. Once

he lay motionless, praying, for hours as rifle-toting soldiers patrolled as close as a yard from him. And then the Hollywood finale: a spectacular dawn rescue by a team of 41 fresh-faced Marines whose average age was 19.

Addressing the crowd gathered at Andrews through a crackling microphone, O'Grady said he would not have survived "if it wasn't for God and the miracle that he blessed me with." In fact, in the days to come O'Grady would consistently play down his own bravery and credit others for his miraculous rescue—the mark, some would say, of a true hero. "All I was was a scared little bunny rabbit, trying to survive," O'Grady insisted. His family, for all their obvi-

ous pride and relief that his ordeal had a happy ending, seemed to agree. "I think he just acted from instinct," says his father, William O'Grady, 56, a radiologist from Alexandria, Virginia, who served two years in the Navy. "Whether that is pure heroism—who knows?"

The day after O'Grady's triumphant return to the U.S., he and 16 family members and friends went to the White House, where they lunched on macadamia-crusted lamb chops and shiitake mushrooms. The flier, who had had his fill of greens during his slog in the Bosnian brush, did have one quibble with the menu. "Excuse me, Mr. President," he said, "if I don't eat my salad."

ANGEL OF HOPE IN HAITI

Tall and fine-boned, her gray hair neatly bobbed, the elderly American passes a group of crudely saddled donkeys and opens the screened front door of Haiti's Hôpital Albert Schweitzer (HAS). As she moves through a sea of patients afflicted with tuberculosis, malaria, typhoid and malnutrition—scourges of a country plagued by poverty—even the sickest turn to catch a glimpse of her. Gwendolyn Mellon, 83, widow of an heir to one of America's greatest fortunes, has reported for work.

Gwen, a trained medical technician, and her husband, Larimer—a scion of the Mellon banking and oil family—opened HAS in 1956 in the village of Deschapelles, 80 miles from the capital, Port-au-Prince. Inspired by a magazine article about Albert Schweitzer's hospital in the African nation of Gabon, they built a charitable facility that eventually earned a reputation as the best hospital in Haiti, nearly eradicating measles and tetanus in the 610-square-mile area it serves. In 1989, as Larry was dying of cancer and Parkinson's disease, he called Gwen to his bedside and asked her to take his place as director of HAS. "I would have died if I hadn't had that responsibility right away," she says, "because we were so close, and we worked so well together."

Gwen Mellon's greatest challenge came during the political crisis of 1994 as a U.S. embargo, designed to force out the junta of Haitian generals, cut off fuel supplies. Gwen called a staff meeting and announced that health facilities around the world operate without electricity and HAS could too. When the U.S. government urged Americans to leave Haiti for their own safety, she stayed. Even in the face of a threatened U.S. invasion—and the potential for reprisals against Americans—she remained fearless. "I had no idea what was going to happen," she says. "But this is my home." Following the return from exile and reinstatement of Haiti's elected president, Jean-Bertrand Aristide, she looks now to the future with hope. "I think this is the most wonderful era in Haiti," she says. "There's peace, and such possibility."

Making the rounds of her hospital, Gwen Mellon checks on Odelange, 7, a motherless child suffering from malnutrition.

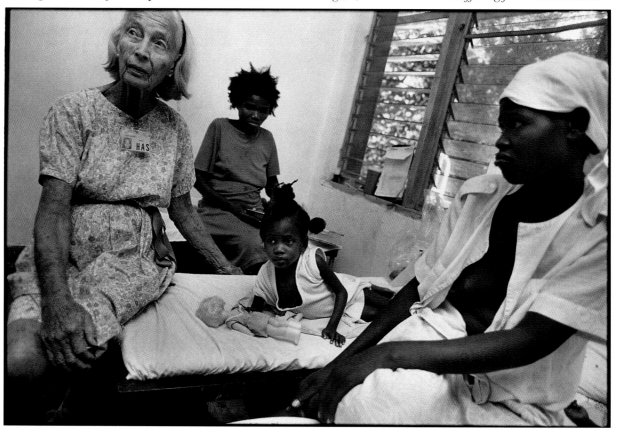

Stephanie Bullock, Oseola McCarty's first scholarship winner, says she'd like to "adopt" the retired washerwoman.

HER SAVING GRACE

For most of her 87 years, Oseola McCarty of Hattiesburg, Mississippi, took in the wash of the local gentry—and did it by hand. McCarty, who tried a washer and dryer but found them woefully inadequate, scrubbed clothes on a washboard in the yard behind the wood-frame house she once shared with her mother and grandmother. The bankers and doctors and lawyers of Hattiesburg (pop. 45,000) considered McCarty a treasure. What they did not know was that McCarty was quietly amassing her own treasure. Then, after arthritis forced the tiny washerwoman to retire, the University of Southern Mississippi in Hattiesburg revealed she was leaving some $150,000 to finance scholarships for African-American students. Says McCarty: "They can have the chance that I didn't have."

McCarty lost her chance in the sixth grade when an unwed aunt came out of the hospital unable to walk. McCarty left school to care for her; she also helped her mother and grandmother with their backyard laundry business. Over the years her fee rose from 50 cents a bundle (a week's worth of laundry for a family of four) to $10. And her needs were few. She does not have a car. She has one TV that works and an air conditioner that she rarely turns on. Mostly, she reads her Bible.

The first Oseola McCarty Scholarship of $1,000 was awarded to Stephanie Bullock, 18, whose mother teaches school in Hattiesburg and whose father supervises a water-treatment plant. "When we heard about the scholarship," says Stephanie, "my mama was smiling from ear to ear." Word of McCarty's gift has, in fact, caused a good many people to smile—and open their pocketbooks. Local businesspeople have pledged to match McCarty's $150,000. McCarty, meanwhile, is a bit bewildered by the question she hears over and over: Why didn't you spend the money on yourself? "I *am* spending it on myself," she answers with the sweetest of smiles.

55

PALADINS &
POLEMICISTS

The world turns, always has, on ideologues. Their message is borne with the fire or guise of faith; it sticks in our heart—or craw. In Bosnia or the Middle East or in the issues that divide America, who's a freedom-fighter and who's a fanatic? To believers in democracy, Harry Wu is clearly on the side of the angels. Having spent two decades as a Chinese political prisoner before immigrating to the U.S., Wu, 58, has several times smuggled video cameras into China's forced labor camps to expose the horrors there. Arrested in June as he tried again to slip through one of China's remote border posts, he was threatened with execution for spying. Then freed after 66 days of captivity, Wu eagerly rejoined his wife, Ching-lee (right), in their Milpitas, California, home but vowed he won't stop blasting China's human rights abuses. "I won't give up," he said. "No way."

Shocked by gangsta rap's sometimes violent, misogynist lyrics, civil rights activist C. DeLores Tucker, 66, urged the record industry to pull the plug on some of its hot-selling rap artists. One target company, Time Warner (parent of PEOPLE), agreed to sell its half interest in the rap label Interscope Records. Proclaimed Tucker: "We have to save these children." The world's most famous political prisoner, Nobel Peace Prizewinner Daw Aung San Suu Kyi (right), 50, was released from house arrest after six years and told her supporters, "We will surely get to our destination if we join hands."

Like an actor in a long-running show, Ronald Reagan continues to play his familiar role—golfing, going to the office—but often forgets his lines. The ex-President, who turned 84, courageously and publicly acknowledged he has Alzheimer's, focusing attention on an incurable brain disease that touches some 4 million Americans. Nancy and he also established a new institute to speed further international research. Below, Bill McCartney, 54, an ex-University of Colorado football coach packed stadiums across the country with weepy all-male rallies of Promise Keepers. A fast-growing evangelical Christian movement, PK preaches marital responsibility, sexual purity and racial harmony. It also stirred controversy with its intolerance of homosexuals and its advocacy of male supremacy.

Fortune smiled on LOTTERY WINNER PAM HIATT, *among numerous luminous others, in '95, but* DAVID LETTERMAN *was among those who had to pucker up and pray for next year*

LADY LUCK

Pam Hiatt—unwed, eight months pregnant and working two part-time jobs while studying at Boise State University in Idaho—had a stupendous reversal of fortune when she won $87 million in the 18-state Powerball lottery. Then, after a jaunt to New York City to appear on *Late Show with David Letterman*, she experienced what she considered the ultimate jackpot: the birth of her first child, Nicholas. "I want him to grow up caring about people and knowing the value of work," says Hiatt, 27. "I want him to realize that everything isn't always handed to you."

SNAKE EYES

David Letterman, 48, the Humpty-Dumpty of the TV mountain, took a tumble in '95. He bombed as Oscars' host and lost his ratings edge over Jay Leno, who also aced him out for the Best Variety Emmy. Envious of guest Hiatt's year, Dave jokingly proposed marriage. Her response: "I was like, 'Okay, let's go!'" But then on reflection, she decided, "I'm holding out for Val Kilmer."

67TH ANNUAL OSCAR AWARDS
(Presented March 27, 1995)
Picture: *Forrest Gump*
Actor: Tom Hanks, *Forrest Gump*
Actress: Jessica Lange, *Blue Sky*
Supporting Actor: Martin Landau, *Ed Wood*
Supporting Actress: Dianne Wiest, *Bullets Over Broadway*
Director: Robert Zemeckis, *Forrest Gump*
Original Screenplay: Quentin Tarantino and Roger Avary, *Pulp Fiction*
Adapted Screenplay: Eric Roth, *Forrest Gump*
Music, Original Song: "Can You Feel the Love Tonight," *The Lion King*
Jean Hersholt Humanitarian Award: Quincy Jones
Irving G. Thalberg Memorial Award: Clint Eastwood
Lifetime Achievement Award: Michelangelo Antonioni

LIZZY GARDINER

Give Lizzy Gardiner credit. American Express does, and the 28-year-old Australian designer appeared at the Academy Awards sheathed in a gown made of 254 Amex gold cards. Gardiner's gilded getup transformed a minor moment—the Oscar for Best Costume Design, which she and her partner, Tim Chappel, won for the drag-queen comedy *Priscilla, Queen of the Desert*—into the show's most visual charge. The attention she has received as a result of the stunt is a novelty to Gardiner, who recently moved from Sydney to Hollywood and laments, "I'm brought down to earth every time I put my hands in my pocket and see I've only got $135."

TOM HANKS

It was a zero gravity year for Tom Hanks. Following his '94 statue for portraying an AIDS-afflicted lawyer in *Philadelphia* with a second for his evocation of the wondrous *Forrest Gump*, Hanks became the first Best Actor since Spencer Tracy to win back-to-back Oscars. Meanwhile he did a voice on Disney's *Toy Story*, and *Apollo 13*, in which he played Commander Jim Lovell, was a box office smash and a personal high for Hanks. "If they said, 'You can go on the shuttle, but you'll have to give two years to train, study and prepare,' I'd gladly do it," he says. "You bet."

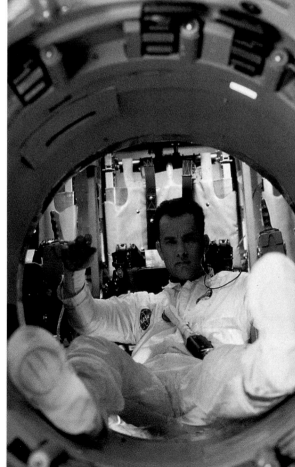

ALAN JACKSON

Honey-voiced Alan Jackson, 36, who stood out among all the big hats at the 1995 Country Music Awards, began wearing a Stetson, he says, "just to cover up this big scar on my forehead where I fell when I was young." One thing Jackson doesn't hide under his hat is his talent. But even though he has had 16 No. 1 singles in recent years, he insists, "I've never been caught up in all of the star stuff. I just make my records and sing. Then, I go home."

29TH ANNUAL COUNTRY MUSIC AWARDS
(Presented October 4, 1995)
Entertainer of the Year: Alan Jackson
Male Vocalist: Vince Gill
Female Vocalist: Alison Krauss
Single: "When You Say Nothing At All," Alison Krauss & Union Station
Album: *When Fallen Angels Fly*, Patty Loveless
Vocal Group: The Mavericks
Vocal Duo: Brooks & Dunn
Music Video: "Baby Likes to Rock It," The Tractors
Horizon Award: Alison Krauss
Song: "Independence Day," Gretchen Peters
Event: Shenandoah with Alison Krauss, "Somewhere in the Vicinity of the Heart"
Musician: Mark O'Connor, fiddle

ALISON KRAUSS

She is the first bluegrass artist to be inducted into the Grand Ole Opry since Jim & Jesse 30 years ago, and her hits' compilation, *Now That I've Found You*, went platinum in 1995. But at age 24, Alison Krauss is still an irreverent sort who loves to just fiddle around. "Wow, you people," she exclaimed on accepting her first trophy at the Country Music Association awards, "I'll never be able to keep my dinner down." By the time country's new diva was called to the podium to accept her fourth award, she was completely flabbergasted. "I'm going to have to get a flask or something," she said. "This is really weird, you guys."

OPRAH WINFREY

Gab goddess Oprah Winfrey, 41, flexed her biceps and extended her empire ever further in 1995. In addition to collecting her and her show's 22nd and 23rd Emmys she signed a deal to produce films for the next five years for Walt Disney Pictures, including an adaptation of Toni Morrison's Pulitzer-Prizewinning novel *Beloved*. She doesn't need the dough. Earlier in the year, *Forbes* put Winfrey on its 400-richest list, declaring that she was "well on her way to becoming America's first black billionaire." In her shadow at the Emmys (above) was her ever steady, Stedman Graham, who's still reaching for the ultimate gold ring.

RENA SOFER

"It's taken me years to look in the mirror and say, 'Yes! I like what I see!'" says Rena Sofer, 25. Modesty aside, it took Sofer just two seasons in her *General Hospital* role as Lois Cerullo, the brassy Brooklyn-bred manager of a rock band, to win an Emmy and help lift the long-running ABC soap out of the ratings doldrums. For the New Jersey-reared daughter of a rabbi and a psychology professor, who split when she was a toddler, playing Lois has been a liberating experience. Says Sofer: "I can yell, scream, cry, fight—and be a child."

KELSEY GRAMMER

Professionally, '95 smiled on Kelsey Grammer, 40. *Frasier* nabbed five Emmys, and he tested movie waters in *Down Periscope* and wrote a memoir, *So Far*. Personally, he was relieved when authorities decided not to indict him on charges of having sex with a teen who baby-sat his daughter. "I look forward to putting all this behind me," he said, though a $20 million civil suit is pending.

Supporting Actress, Comedy Series: Christine Baranski, *Cybill*
Supporting Actor, Miniseries or Special: Donald Sutherland, *Citizen X*
Supporting Actress, Miniseries or Special: (tie) Judy Davis, *Serving in Silence: The Margarethe Cammermeyer Story*; and Shirley Knight, *Indictment: The McMartin Trial*
Individual Performance, Variety or Music Show: Barbra Streisand, *Barbra Streisand The Concert*

49TH ANNUAL TONY AWARDS
(Presented June 4, 1995)
Play: *Love! Valour! Compassion!,* Terrence McNally
Musical: *Sunset Boulevard*
Actor, Play: Ralph Fiennes, *Hamlet*
Actress, Play: Cherry Jones, *The Heiress*
Actor, Musical: Matthew Broderick, *How to Succeed in Business Without Really Trying*
Actress, Musical: Glenn Close, *Sunset Boulevard*
Featured Actor, Play: John Glover, *Love! Valor! Compassion!*
Featured Actress, Play: Frances Sternhagen, *The Heiress*
Featured Actor, Musical: George Hearn, *Sunset Boulevard*
Featured Actress, Musical: Gretha Boston, *Show Boat*
Revival, Play: *The Heiress*
Revival, Musical: *Show Boat*

GLENN CLOSE & BARBRA STREISAND

On top of collecting five Emmys for her HBO special *Barbra Streisand The Concert*, Streisand, 53, produced *Serving in Silence: The Margarethe Cammermeyer Story*, the compelling NBC docudrama about a lesbian Army officer, which earned Glenn Close her first award for a performance on film, after numerous previous Oscar and Emmy nominations. "I'm a great believer in the power of television," proclaimed Close, 48, who was honored earlier in the year for her bravura evocation of Norma Desmond in the Broadway musical *Sunset Boulevard*.

TOM PETTY

Tom Petty was 11 when he met Elvis Presley, who was filming *Follow That Dream* near Gainesville, Florida. Petty soon traded his slingshot for a stack of Presley 45s and began following his own dream with a Sears mail-order guitar. In 1995, Petty, 45, racked up sales of more than $2 million for his *Wildflowers* album and was the elder statesman at the MTV Awards. "That drive to be king," he says, "is an instinct that we all seem to have."

TLC

The libidinous R&B of TLC—(from left), Tionne "T-Boz" Watkins, 25, Lisa "Left Eye" Lopes, 23, and Rozonda "Chili" Thomas, 24—won the group super kudos at the 1995 MTV Music Video Awards. But two weeks after their *CrazySexyCool* album went triple platinum, Lopes—who is serving five years' probation for trying to burn the house of her beau, Cleveland Browns star Andre Rison—and her singing partners filed for bankruptcy. Clearly these girls are in need of some Tender Loving Care.

SHERYL CROW

True to her avian surname, Sheryl Crow, 31, saw her career soar in 1995. The former backup singer for Michael Jackson and Don Henley followed her rousing appearance at Woodstock '94 with three Grammys. Crow, who has suffered from extreme depression in the past, still wrestles with occasional mood downturns. "Only now," she says, "I know it's going to go away."

GREEN DAY

When the neo-punk group Green Day performs in the San Francisco Bay area, where they got their start, some punk fans seem less than pleased that these local boys have made good. "Sellouts!" they heckle. "Green Day sucks!" The feeling is hardly unanimous. Green Day's major-label debut, *Dookie* (slang for excrement), sold more than 6 million copies, earned a Grammy and drop-kicked the three 22-year-olds—(from left) bassist Mike Dirnt, singer-guitarist Billie Joe Armstrong and drummer Tré Cool—from obscurity to the top of the pop charts. Exults San Francisco deejay Steve Masters: "They have that awesome punk rock energy that makes me want to smash beer bottles on my head."

37TH ANNUAL GRAMMY AWARDS
(Presented March 1, 1995)
Record of the Year: "All I Wanna Do," Sheryl Crow
Song of the Year: "Streets of Philadelphia," Bruce Springsteen
Album of the Year: *MTV Unplugged,* Tony Bennett
New Artist: Sheryl Crow
Male Pop Vocal: "Can You Feel the Love Tonight," Elton John
Female Pop Vocal: "All I Wanna Do," Sheryl Crow
Pop Vocal by a Duo or Group: "I Swear," All 4 One
Traditional Pop Performance: "MTV Unplugged," Tony Bennett
Rock Song: "Streets of Philadelphia," Bruce Springsteen
Male Rock Vocal: "Streets of Philadelphia," Bruce Springsteen
Female Rock Vocal: "Come to My Window," Melissa Etheridge
Rock Vocal by a Duo or Group: "Crazy," Aerosmith
R&B Song: "I'll Make Love to You," Babyface
Male R&B Vocal: "When Can I See You," Babyface
Female R&B Vocal: "Breathe Again," Toni Braxton
R&B Vocal by a Duo or Group: "I'll Make Love to You," Boyz II Men
Rap Solo: "U.N.I.T.Y.," Queen Latifah
Rap Performance by a Duo or Group: "None of Your Business," Salt 'N Pepa
Hard Rock Performance: "Black Hole Sun," Soundgarden
Metal Performance: "Spoonman," Soundgarden
Alternative Music Album: *Dookie,* Green Day

MAKING THE GUYS SALUTE

If guys are endlessly inspired by the Gipper, maybe the women of late are winning one for the Faulkner, Shannon that is. At West Point—193 years after the Academy was founded and 19 years after it began accepting females—Rebecca Marier, 21, became the first woman to graduate at the top of the cadet class. "People better get ready," she declared, "because there are a lot of talented women behind me." Meanwhile, for the first time in the 144-year history of the Americas Cup, the most-prized trophy in world-class sailing, a yacht crewed by women (including, below, Shelley Beattie, grinding away) nearly made it to the finals. Though *America³*—an all women-plus-one-man team who dubbed their boat "Mighty Mary"—blew a five-minute lead in a final race with former Americas Cup champion Dennis Connor and lost their chance to compete against Team New Zealand, they earned respect in the staid, male-dominated world of yacht racing. Says *America³* team boss Bill Koch: "They were no longer viewed as the girls, but those SOBs on Mighty Mary."

"I had a lot of dreams about making a difference in the world," says Rebecca Marier (with Army Chief of Staff Gordon Sullivan during the West Point graduation ceremonies).

WOMEN ON THE MOVE

Three golden girls of 1995 were tender only in years. Nicole Bobek, 17, crossed rough ice—eight coaches and as many addresses in eight years—to become U.S. Figure Skating Champion. Rebecca Lobo, 22, led her UConn Huskies to a perfect season. And Tiffany Roberts, 18, was the youngest of the defending world champ U.S women's soccer team that got whupped by Norway but did take the bronze.

Net star Rebecca Lobo was so popular in Connecticut that she was asked and demurred about running for office. "Sorry," she says, "half of the people hate you, and I don't want that. Besides, I don't lie well enough to be a politician."

THUMBS DOWN FOR A HEXED TRIO

Disgraced Olympic skater Tonya Harding tried to reinvent herself as a pop diva and instead was treated to yet another public mugging. At a concert in Portland, Oregon, Harding kicked off with an original song: "Feel the beat," she sang, "feel the heat." Mostly what she and her Golden Blades group felt was the derision of 10,000 raucous music festival fans, who forced them off the stage with a barrage of boos and bottles. Al Harding, Tonya's father, tried to be philosophical. "You can't please all the people all the time," he said. But Tonya, on three years' probation for covering up her and her ex-husband Jeff Gillooly's involvement in the 1994 attack on rival Nancy Kerrigan, got little sympathy from anyone else. "I want my $3 back," said one concertgoer after the Golden Blades performance. "And I didn't even pay."

SUSAN POWTER

Money, not fat, is Susan Powter's biggest problem these days. The "Stop the Insanity!" infomercial queen, who struck it rich with her weight-loss videos and books, looked like she was in for another blockbuster year in 1995 after launching a weekday TV talk show and pocketing a $2 million advance for her third book, *Food*. But even though her company was reportedly raking in nearly $1 million a week, Powter, 37, lamented that she was unable to pay her bills. She filed for personal bankruptcy, claiming she had been wiped out by legal fees resulting from a feud with her business partners, Gerald and Richard Frankel. Having once gone from fat to thin, the crew-cut flab buster now faces a new challenge: Stop the Insolvency.

NICK LEESON

It took 233 years for Britain's Barings Bank to amass $9.37 billion in assets. But Nick Leeson, 28, a rogue trader in its Singapore office, needed only two months to send the institution that financed Britain's wars against Napoleon (1798-1815) hurtling into bankruptcy and disgrace. Unbeknownst to Barings' officers, Leeson wagered billions of pounds in Asian financial markets, betting that Japanese stock indexes would rise. When they fell, the bank was unable to pony up the estimated $1.1 billion Leeson had lost. A clerk before Barings hired him in 1989, Leeson seemed to undergo a personality transformation as he became a high-rolling master of the universe. He was once fined $138 for exposing himself at a Singapore disco. Another time he was hauled in for disorderly conduct, but Barings reportedly got the charges dropped. It was a move it likely now regrets. "Soul-destroying," is how one member of the Baring clan described the bank's crash.

DUAL CAREERS SPLIT A FAIRY-TALE COUPLE

The ballad of **LYLE LOVETT** *and his pretty woman,* **JULIA ROBERTS**, *ends with a sad refrain in a tough year for celeb wedlock*

"Can you doubt we were made for each other?" Lyle Lovett once sang to Julia Roberts. After 21 months in semiabsentia, the answer, unhappily, was yes. When Roberts, 27, and Lovett, 37, announced their separation, there was no explanation, just a claim of mutual goodwill. Said the couple: "We remain close and in great support of each other."

From the very beginning of the Julia-Lyle fairy tale—beautiful-but-vulnerable movie star falls big for offbeat country crooner—wishful thinking seems to have had an edge over dour common sense. For starters, when they met in June 1993, both Julia and Lyle were on the rebound from failed romances—hers with Jason Patric, his with Allison Inman. Married on June 27, 1993, just three weeks after they met—the barefoot bride wore a plain white sheath, the groom a dark suit and a crooked grin—the two professed deep love. Pulling his bride onstage in Noblesville, Indiana, hours after their wedding, Lovett said, "Welcome to the happiest day of my life."

But one happy day does not a lifetime make. The fact is, for all their love-struck proclamations, Lovett and Roberts pledged till-death-do-them-part to virtual strangers. And taking time to get to know each other proved to be something the couple either could not—or would not—do. The day after the wedding, Roberts flew back to Washington to finish filming *The Pelican Brief,* and Lovett resumed his concert tour. During the next 21 months, the couple rarely spent more than a week at a time together and, in fact, kept separate residences: hers a co-op in New York City, his a clapboard farmhouse in Klein, Texas (pop. 12,000). Still, as they saw it, their love was strong enough to withstand the lack of togetherness. "We are pretending to be a normal couple," Roberts said of their moments together.

For every Hallmark moment, however, came a Scene from an Unhappy Marriage. In April 1994, when their schedules brought them briefly and simultaneously to New York City, Roberts and Lovett stayed at separate hotels. Several days later, with Lyle back in Paris shooting his *Ready to Wear* scenes, Julia was photographed in a tight squeeze on the dance floor of a Manhattan restaurant with actor Ethan Hawke. Roberts and Lovett spent their first anniversary apart. She was in Manhattan doing press for *I Love Trouble;* he was in L.A. working on a video for his *I Love Everybody* album. Asked then about the state of her marriage, the giddy girl of the year before was gone, replaced by a wiser, more ambivalent young woman. "Basically, what it comes down to," said Roberts, "is what time you spend [together], you try to make it the best you can."

Lovett too began to show signs of weariness. At a concert in Buffalo in December 1994, a voice from the back of the room shouted, "Where's Julia?" Lovett replied, "She's . . . she's everywhere." But just a few weeks before the separation, after he and Roberts spent Valentine's Day together, Lovett was wearing his rose-colored glasses. "Life is a lot more normal than what people might think from keeping up with the tabloid media," he said. "I'm just really happy to be in a great relationship."

Ironically the sad news of the breakup may be good news for some of Lyle's fans. "It's harder to write songs when you're happy than it is when you're miserable," Lovett once said. "Who wants to hear how happy you are?"

ONCE GA GA, NOW ZSA ZSA

A bad marriage is like a volcano. Some send off so many smoke signals that the final eruption is no surprise. Others blow all at once, burying the surrounding countryside in a blanket of dust or a tabloid blizzard. In a better year for the tabs than for togetherness in the Celebrity Nation, Liz Taylor decided apparently that eight isn't enough. For four years, Taylor seemed to have found a kind of calm in the low-key company of the twice-divorced Larry Fortensky, who drives an off-road Caterpillar dirt compactor for a living. But Fortensky, 43, apparently got fed up with having to nurse his cranky, 63-year-old bride through her hip replacement operations. Now, as far as Liz is concerned, Larry will have to make the earth move on his day job.

Michael Douglas, 51, often succumbed to basic instincts during his 18-year marriage to his documentary producer wife, Diandra, 37. "The other women," Diandra once said, "were difficult to deal with." He claimed it was playing sexually driven characters that led to false rumors that he was a sex addict. Diandra filed for divorce, asking for joint custody of their 15-year-old son, Cameron.

Forget forever, Batman. The vows taken seven years ago by Val Kilmer, 35, and Joanne Whalley, 33, star of the 1994 Scarlett *mini-series, turned out to be transient as she sought divorce and custody of their two children. Jim Carrey's wife Melissa, 35, got $3.5 million, plus $35,000 monthly (their daughter is 8) when they finalized their split. Carrey, 33, now lives with actress Lauren Holly. Matt Lattanzi, 36, had been supportive through the recovery of Olivia Newton-John, 46, after a partial mastectomy, but couples therapy could not resolve their differences. Matt was a backup dancer when they met in 1979 filming* Xanadu; *they have one daughter.*

PARTINGS 1995

The 23-year on-again, off-again romance between *Melanie Griffith*, 37, and *Don Johnson*, 45, was officially off again when they ended their second marriage after six years and one daughter.

Former Led Zeppelin guitarist *Jimmy Page*, 51, and model *Patricia Ecker*; after nine years and one son.

Fresh Prince star *Will Smith* and wife *Sheree*, both 26; after three years and one son.

Actress *Mariette Hartley*, 54, and husband *Patrick Boyriven*, 57, a producer-director; after 16 years and three children.

Tough guy actor *James Caan*, 55, and third wife *Ingrid*, 34; after four years and one son.

Actress *Barbara Rush*, 65, and public relations czar *Warren Cowan*, 74; after five years.

Picket Fences' Judge Bone, *Ray Walston*, 80, and wife *Ruth*, 79; after 51 years.

A day after *Sylvester Stallone*, split with model *Angie Everhart*, 25, his fiancée of three months, he was snuggling with model-actress Jennifer Flavin, an ex-girlfriend he had dumped via a letter sent Federal Express in 1994.

Home Improvement's Patricia Richardson, 44, and *Under Suspicion's* Ray Baker, 47; after 13 years and three kids.

*Kevin Costne*r, 40, and his wife *Cindy*, 39; after 17 years and three children.

PARTINGS 1995

Cheryl Tiegs, 48, and her husband, actor-writer *Anthony Peck*, 39; after five years and one son.

Lee Iacocca, 71, and his wife, *Darrien Earle*, 56; after four years.

Former Olympic figure skater *Dorothy Hamill*, 39, and husband, *Kenneth Forsythe*, 51, a sports physician; after eight years and one child.

Romance novel queen *Danielle Steel*, 48, and her fourth husband, former shipping magnate *John Traina*, 61; separated after 14 years and five children.

Actress *Beverly D'Angelo*, 43, filed for divorce from her estranged husband, *Lorenzo Salviati*, an Italian businessman. They wed in 1981 and separated in 1985.

TV regular *James Brolin*, 54, and wife *Jan Smithers*, 45, from *WKRP in Cincinnati;* after nine years and one daughter.

Christian Slater, 25, and his fiancée, *Nina Huang*, 32; after five years together.

Actor *Ralph Fiennes*, 32, and actress *Alex Kingston*, 31; separated after two years.

British actor *John Hurt*, 55, and his third wife, *Jo Dalton,* 36; after five years of marriage and two sons.

Ex-James Bond star *Roger Moore*, 67, and third wife, *Luisa*, 56; after 27 years and three children.

Charging that his wife hokeypokeyed with another man, Robert Duvall, 64, filed for divorce from Shannon Brophy, a 30-something dance instructor he had met at a tango class in 1986. Patriot Games author Tom Clancy, 48, split, then reconciled with Wanda, 46, his wife of 25 years and mother of his four kids; she had accused him of adultery with Katherine "Ping Ping" Huang, 26, a Bronx assistant district attorney he met over the Internet.

Married six years, Britain's Golden Couple, actor-director Kenneth Branagh, 34, and actress Emma Thompson, 36, functioned more as two separate nuggets of late and split after spending only 100 days of the year together.

Tommy Lee Jones (above), 48, broke with Kimberlea, 37, his wife of 14 years, after falling for a 31-year-old camera assistant. Uptown Girl Christie Brinkley (right), 42, split with Outdoor Guy Ricky Taubman, 46, after just eight months. And Anthony Quinn, 80, got the boot after 29 years from Iolanda, 60, for his philandering ways.

PARTINGS 1995

Phil Collins, 44, and his wife *Jill,* 39; after 11 years and one daughter.

Richard Gere, 46, and *Cindy Crawford*, 29; after four years.

Singer-actress *Shirley Jones*, 61, separated from comedian-agent *Marty Ingels*, 59; after 17 years.

Roger Moore, 67, James Bond emeritus, and wife *Luisa*, 56; after 27 years and three kids.

Country singer *Tracy Lawrence*, 27, and wife *Frances*, 26; after two years.

Whoopi Goldberg, fortysomething, and *Lyle Trachtenberg*, 41, a union organizer; after one year. Romance had reportedly bloomed between Whoopi and her costar in the upcoming film *Eddie*, *Frank Langella*, 55, who split with his wife *Ruth Weil*, 54; after 18 years and two children.

Kung Fu's *David Carradine*, 59, separated from his producer-songwriter wife *Gail Jensen*, 46; after seven years.

NYPD Blue's *Nicholas Turturro*, 33, and wife *Jami*, 31; after nearly a dozen years and one daughter.

Singer *Natalie Cole*, and music producer *André Fischer;* after almost three years.

The Wonder Years' *Jason Hervey*, 23, and wife *Kelley Patricia O'Neill*, 28; after 19 months.

Hall of Fame baseball catcher *Johnny Bench*, 47, and wife *Laura,* 32; after seven years.

SIX WHO GOT THEIRS

In a year when guys began belatedly to get it, a few actually got theirs, including Sen. Robert Packwood, 63. For 27 years the Oregon Republican championed women's rights while, in private, he did women wrong. Recalling the day he forcibly kissed her, former aide Paige Wagers says: "I could feel my skin crawl." Accused of groping at least 19 women and shamed by released private diary entries detailing also his tightness with lobbyists, Packwood offered no apologies when he resigned. "I leave this institution not with malice," he said, "but with love."

One month after reporting W.R. Grace & Co.'s best earnings in a decade, J.P. Bolduc, 55, abruptly resigned as president and CEO. "Alleged abusive behavior with females affiliated with the company began to surface," explained J. Peter Grace Jr., chairman of the conglomerate. Cheered Kathryn Rogers of the NOW Legal Defense and Education Fund: "This is the first time that a company has taken the action of having a CEO leave because of sexual harassment."

Nobel laureate Aleksandr Solzhenitsyn's talk show career proved even shorter than Pat Sajak's. A year after the debut of Russian TV's A Meeting with Solzhenitsyn, it was axed because of low ratings. Solzhenitsyn, 76, who returned home in 1994 after 18 years in the U.S., used the program as a platform for rants about Russia's shameful moral condition.

It was anchors away for Connie Chung, 49, at the CBS Evening News, leaving Dan Rather alone again. Some claimed that CBS had unfairly blamed her for the Evening News' poor ratings and had tarnished her reputation by forcing her to court sensational subjects like Tonya Harding for Eye to Eye. Others contended that Chung was a bantamweight who embarrassed CBS with gambits like the Eye to Eye interview in which she persuaded Kathleen Gingrich to reveal "just between you and me" that her son Newt deemed Hillary Clinton a "bitch." Four days following her ouster, Connie got better news: After years of struggling to have a child, she and her husband, talk show host Maury Povich, 56, learned they were about to become adoptive parents of a baby boy.

William Agee, 57, who won notoriety in 1980 at Bendix when he promoted wife-to-be Mary Cunningham to VP, was forced out after six years as chairman of Morrison Knudsen, a struggling construction company, for a self-aggrandizing management style. And Winnie Mandela, 60, got axed from the cabinet of her estranged husband, South African President Nelson Mandela, amid allegations that she had been using her post as Deputy Minister of Art, Culture and Science for financial gain.

CHAMPS WHO HUNG IT UP

Joe Montana, who engineered 31 fourth-quarter comeback victories as an NFL quarterback, once told his teammates near the end of a close game: "Don't worry about the clock, don't listen to the crowd, and let's have some fun." Such consummate cool helped Montana lead the San Francisco '49ers to four Super Bowl titles and made him perhaps the greatest NFL quarterback ever. Thus, it was fitting, as he wound down his 16-year pro career at 38, that he once again refused to be beaten by the clock. No, he insisted, he wasn't retiring because he had no cartilage in his left knee and his four kids (including Nathaniel, 6, right) were afraid to jump on old dad. No, he wasn't bowing to pressure from his wife, Jennifer. The real reason in Joe's touching words: "A day comes along, you wake up and realize it isn't as much of a game as it once was, that it feels like a job. I always told myself that would be the time to retire."

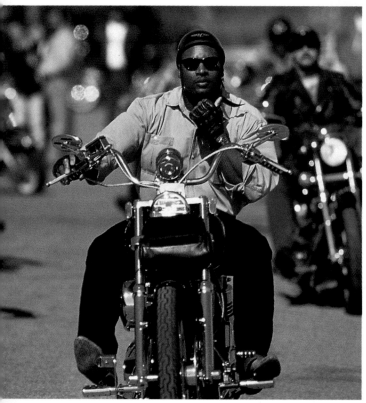

Everybody used to know Bo Jackson, the pre-Deion, two-sport phenom who was an NFL Pro Bowler as well as a baseball All-Star not to mention Nike's main man. After valiantly continuing in baseball when a hip injury ended his football career in 1991, he finally hopped on his hog at age 32 and moved on. Hubert de Givenchy, 68, the Frenchman who modernized high-end couture, and dressed the ever-elegant Audrey Hepburn, presented his last collection in '95. "I'm afraid it's an insult to say this," he mused, "but you must understand that an era is finished."

Dorothy Hamill, 38, who won a gold medal at the 1976 Olympics, hung up her figure skates and sold the Ice Capades, which she had acquired in 1993.

Though often touted as a future Democratic presidential candidate, three-term New Jersey Sen. *Bill Bradley,* 52, announced he had grown weary of a political system that is "broken," and would not stand for reelection in 1996. Said Bradley: "Neither political party speaks to people where they live their lives."

Arguing that voices of common sense had been "drowned out by the extremes in both parties," Georgia Sen. *Sam Nunn*, 57, the leading Democratic expert on military affairs, said he did not have the "zest and enthusiasm" to seek a fifth term.

And after them, a deluge of other Senate and House incumbents also set their own term limits, announcing that they would not run in '96. Among them was 12-term Colorado Democratic Rep. *Patricia Schroeder*, 55. Outspoken on women's issues, she left a typically facetious epitaph: "I've always been hard to paper-train."

Robert MacNeil, 64, co-anchor of PBS's The Mac-Neil/Lehrer NewsHour *marked the show's 20th anniversary by retiring. Besides working on his third novel, MacNeil said, "I can go to the movies at noon. And I don't have to wait until after 7 p.m. to have a drink." After collecting six Olympic gold medals, Bonnie Blair, 31, ended her skating career by winning the 1995 World Cup and World Sprint titles at 500 and 1,000 meters. Asked if there were anything else she wished she had accomplished, she responded, "Not a thing, thank you."*

LOOK OF THE YEAR

FASHIONS TO KEEP THE STARS IN STITCHES

Creating clothes both goofy and glamorous, **CYNTHIA ROWLEY** *was the designer of choice in a year when tastes ran from pink to the Pitt*

As one of Seventh Avenue's fastest-rising stars, designer Cynthia Rowley would naturally aspire to be as big as Calvin Klein or Donna Karan. But Ron Popeil? "He's *totally* my idol," says Rowley, 37, of the inventor-cum-TV-hockmeister who became famous selling everything from Popeil's Pocket Fisherman to aerosol hair. Recently, Rowley literally dreamed up a new gadget. "I can't say what it is, in case I really do it," she says. "Not that I want to get out of making clothes. But it was so good I woke up saying, 'This is my ticket out of here!'"

But why should Rowley get out when she has just arrived with such éclat? Regarded as a consummate tailor, she was named the best new talent of the year in 1995 by the Council of Fashion Designers of America. She specializes in nostalgically lighthearted styles, such as lemon-patterned hostess gowns and shirtwaists in her trademark plaids, which are both comfortable and affordable. Says Rowley with pride: "I don't design for elitists." Hip celebs, though, are among her biggest fans. Sarah Jessica Parker and *The Nanny*'s Fran Drescher wear her dresses, and Christie Brinkley schussed in a Rowley skirt at her 1994 Telluride ski-slope nuptials to Ricky Taubman. "I love her clothes," says actress Clare (*My So-Called Life*) Danes, who modeled in her spring show. "They're a nice mix between funky and wearable—not too serious." Sort of

"Fashion is too serious," says a statuesque Rowley, who designed a wedding dress for Christie Brinkley, as well as the clothes worn by Clare Danes (middle) and Natalie Merchant at the 1995 MTV Music Video Awards show.

like Rowley herself. "She is a combination of Audrey Hepburn, Mary Tyler Moore and Gidget," says Katie Couric, "and the least intimidating person in fashion."

Rowley got her first big break while studying design at the Art Institute of Chicago in the late '70s, when she was stopped on the subway by a buyer from Marshall Field who admired the cropped khaki jacket she had created on the sewing machine she kept in her dorm room. Within days, Rowley landed a $1,200 order from the store. By 1983 she was running her own business in Manhattan. "Back then, so many things were by the skin of my teeth," she says. "I remember having to count pennies to get on a subway to take the line to show Lord & Taylor."

Expecting sales over $15 million this year, Rowley—a die-hard *I Love Lucy* fan—runs her showroom with sitcom zeal. Clad in one of her funky dresses, she roars up to work on a Suzuki motorcycle and greets her 30 employees by blowing reveille on her bugle. She has been known to strip down to her Fred Flintstone underwear so that a client like rocker Natalie Merchant can try on the dress she is wearing.

A bungee jumper and scuba diver, Rowley shares a Greenwich Village loft with her fiancé Bill Keenan, 42, a retail store designer. (Her photographer husband Tom Sullivan died of cancer at age 32.) She already has additional stores in Chicago and Tokyo and plans for 10 more. In a business rife with burnout and bankruptcy, Rowley says she is "pathologically optimistic." After all, there's that secret invention to fall back on. "Even if I lost it all, I wouldn't be bitter," she says. "If the ceiling fell in tomorrow, I'd say, 'Oh, good, I always wanted a skylight.'"

THINK PINK

"I wouldn't presume to tell a woman what a woman ought to think," said actress Kay Thompson, portraying Maggie Prescott, a fashion editor modeled after *Vogue*'s Diana Vreeland, in the 1957 movie *Funny Face*. "But tell her if she's got to think, think pink!" Now, 40 years later, the fashion world is again heeding that advice, pushing everything from bubblegum-colored handbags to formfitting fuchsia suits. "Pink can work for every personality," says designer Cynthia Rowley, whose pale pink creations have satisfied the palettes of Sarah Jessica Parker, model Stephanie Seymour and singer Lisa Loeb. "It can be sexy, it can be sophisticated, it can be a little trampy."

Thanks to all its high-profile supporters, the hue was everywhere in '95. And that helped designers promote a more feminine look. Says couturier Bill Blass, whose spring collection included a garden of rose-tinted cashmere coats, marabou boleros and silk crepe gowns: "It was my natural reaction after so many seasons of black, black, black. It was a way of poking fun at the fashion industry."

But, style arbiters contend, there's nothing incorrect, sisterhood-wise, about the trend. "Though pink is the color associated with sweetness and femininity," says Valerie Steele, a professor at New York City's Fashion Institute of Technology, "women are now able to wear it without being stereotyped as little froufrou ladies." In fact, declares Blass, wearers must have "a certain sophistication" to be pretty in pink today. "It's insipid on a too-girlish woman," he says. "It needs a little toughness."

Celebs everywhere—including Nicole Kidman (at Cannes), Liza Minnelli (in Hollywood) and Hillary Clinton (at a Massachusetts health clinic)— basked in the glow of pink in 1995.

Leeza Gibbons (at the Daytime Emmys) and Vendela (at the Academy Awards, right) were both tickled pink in formal evening wear. Princess Diana flew her true hue in Canterbury for members of the Princess of Wales Regiment. And even a few fresh guys have gotten into the act: That's Will Smith making a princely entrance at the Batman Forever *premiere* in Los Angeles.

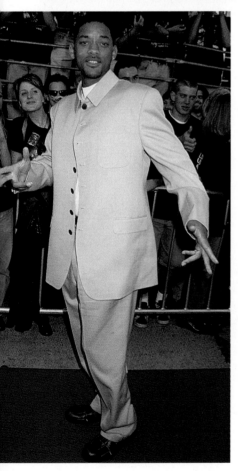

THE SUAVE & THE CLUELESS

George Clooney's prescription for fashion success: Take a suit, a vest, a T-shirt, a Julius Caesar haircut and an off-center smile. Prognosis: a laid-back look that raised female pulses and made the *ER* star one of 1995's Best Dressed People. Style-watchers were awestruck by the figure but not the fashion sense of *Baywatch* beauty Pamela (Anderson) Lee, who wed rocker Tommy Lee last February. The dominatrix outfit and barbed-wire biceps tattoo that Pam sported at Cannes clinched her selection as one of the year's Worst Dressed.

SEÑOR SEXY, BRAD PITT

It's not as though Brad Pitt, 31, PEOPLE's sexiest man of 1995, snuck up on us. You could hardly overlook him in *Thelma & Louise*, where he was the most lustrous mammal of the Golden West. Your pulse stopped at every sun-dappled close-up in *A River Runs Through It*. In *Interview with the Vampire*, you wanted to ride bareback down the slopes of his hair. By *Legends of the Fall*, where Pitt played a tormented member of a western clan, we knew what to expect. "Sinking below, rising above, going off, giving up, taking charge, taking control" is how he described his character. The culmination came in his homicide cop role in *Seven*, which his presence turned into one of the year's sleeper smashes. The film also

introduced him to his lady of the moment, actress Gwyneth Paltrow, 22.

"He's a regular Joe," declares brother Doug, 28, a computer-company owner who, like the rest of the close-knit Pitts, still lives in the shadow of the Ozarks in Springfield, Missouri. (Dad Bill is a trucking-company exec, mom Jane a school counselor.) Yet Doug says that his older brother also has an independent streak. "If the rush was for everyone to go out and buy Harleys," he says, "Brad wouldn't." Perhaps this explains why Pitt avoids playing pretty boys onscreen and downplays his looks off, hiding under a grunged-out wardrobe and knitted cap. "Heartthrobs," Pitt once said, "are a dime a dozen."

FAMILY MATTERS

A DELICATE DÉTENTE AT THE PALACE

Undeterred by that troubled trinity— **DIANA, CHARLES** *and* **CAMILLA—** *Chynna wed, Retton gave birth and hope lived*

For much of the year, it had seemed as though the scandal-torn Windsors had managed to hammer out a thoroughly civilized modus vivendi. Coping, like many clans, with the pain of marital breakdown, they remained in separate orbits but were guided by a rare pragmatism and a rekindled sense of duty.

Putting aside her rebelliousness, the Princess of Wales returned to work, gracefully oblivious to the fact that her estranged husband not only was stepping out with divorcée Camilla Parker Bowles, 48, but also was linked by the tabloids to Tiggy Legge-Bourke, 30, the assistant who serves as nanny to Princes William and Harry. Happy to have Diana, 34, back in her role as the family's most glamorous ambassador, Charles, 47, seemed content to hold off on a divorce—which, of course, would force the issue of whether he will remarry.

In the meantime, Prince Andrew, 35, and the repentant Fergie, 36, took daughters Bea, 7, and Eugenie, 5, on a Spanish holiday, fueling hopes that they may reconcile. And the Queen encouraged Prince Edward, 31, to court his prospective bride chez Windsor—allowing Sophie Rhys-Jones, 30 (a Di doppelganger who has quarters near Edward's at Buckingham Palace) to learn the ropes before joining the Family Firm.

Then, suddenly, in mid-November, Diana "plunged the monarchy into the greatest crisis since the Abdication," in the words of one London newspaper. Inviting the BBC into Kensington Palace for an astonishingly frank taped interview, she portrayed herself as an innocent struggling with a voracious press, vindictive courtiers and the breakdown of a marriage that she had "desperately wanted to work." Yes, she had made cry-for-help suicide attempts (remember the lemon peeler?) and struggled with bulimia; and yes, she had taken refuge in the arms of James Hewitt, 37, an ex-Life Guards officer rumored to possess a cache of billets-doux signed by Di. But who could blame her? Her "woman's instinct" told her that Charles was consorting with Parker Bowles—a betrayal that left her feeling "useless and hopeless and failed." (She was crushed again, she said, when Hewitt collaborated on a bodice-ripping memoir about their affair: "I minded very much," she said, "that [he] made money out of me.")

Aired on the eve of a high-profile working trip to Argentina, Di's dramatic interview was interpreted as a challenge to Charles, whom, she said, she had no desire to divorce—and who, she suggested, has doubts about stepping into the role of king. It was also seen as an attempt to restore the Mother Teresa credentials tarnished by her summer flirtation with rugby captain Will Carling, who befriended her sons. Although she acknowledged a fling with Hewitt, she brushed off a question about married art dealer Oliver Hoare (reportedly her lover) and managed never to discuss Carling—whose wife had blamed her when they split in September. By the time the interview was over, the common folk had rallied behind Diana: In polls taken immediately afterward, 46 percent said that it had made them feel more sympathetic towards Diana, and 74 percent said that they approved of her telling her story.

But if the public sided with Di, the Windsors regarded her TV appearance as "an Exocet aimed at the palace," in the words of Brian Hoey, author of a dozen books on the royals.

Although they had taken pains to relaunch her on the ribbon-cutting circuit, the Queen and her advisers came to view Diana as a "grimly determined adversary," in the words of the *Daily Telegraph*. If there were a silver lining, as they saw it, it was the fact that opinion-makers were now calling for a divorce—which would make Charles look dutiful, rather than heartless, should he end the marriage.

Palace watchers, at least, were not surprised when the Queen threw down the gauntlet. After it was reported that Diana had declined an invitation to spend Christmas with the family at Sandringham, Buckingham Palace made an extraordinary announcement—revealing that the Queen had written to both Charles and Diana, asking them to come to terms on a divorce. Accepting Diana's challenge that Charles take responsibility for a final split, the Palace declared that the Prince, did, in fact, want their 14-year marriage to end.

Keenly aware of Di's position as the mother of the heir and the spare, the monarch will be compelled to treat her delicately. In the wake of the BBC interview, the Palace issued a public offer to "meet with the Princess to see how we can help her define her future . . . and support her"—a strong hint that some kind of goodwill ambassadorship was in the offing. In any case, Diana, herself, seemed to harbor few illusions about preserving the unhappy marriage. In the BBC interview, she admitted that she expected to become Queen only "of people's hearts."

The remaining question, of course, is whether the Windsors can continue to pull together or whether they will become a house tragically divided. After her BBC soul-baring, a then confident Diana seemed to hope that there would be a place for everyone at the Queen's table. "I have no regrets," she told the *Daily Mirror*. "Now I am looking forward to my future."

Infidelity (real and imagined) was a theme for the Waleses: Fleet Street suggested that his sons' nanny Tiggy Legge-Bourke (left, in London) shed weight because she was being romanced by Charles, but insiders discounted the rumors. After Di told the BBC that she was wounded by his 1994 tell-all, James Hewitt (below), retorted, "I feel totally used by Diana."

Although the Queen (at a Parliament opening) was distressed by Diana's confessions to the BBC, she "was more saddened than angered," says British journalist Brian Hoey, who covers the Palace. "Both she and the Royal Family feel that Diana needs help." For all of that, insiders say that Diana (below, at August VE-day anniversary celebrations with Harry, William and Charles) will be unable to retain her standing as a good mother—which is her trump card—if she continues to make sensational revelations about her love life. "As they get older," says a veteran Palace watcher, "William and Harry will question more and more what has gone on. They'll suffer from her admission of infidelity."

THE BELLS WERE RINGING

When the clans of actor William Baldwin, 32, and singer Chynna Phillips, 27, were joined in matrimony, even the guests came to ogle. "All the gorgeous Baldwin brothers were there," says Chynna's dress designer Vera Wang of the groom and his actor sibs, Stephen, Daniel and Alec (with his very pregnant wife, Kim Basinger). "That was enough for me." Chynna's divorced parents, Mamas and Papas founders John and Michelle Phillips, escorted her down the aisle, and her half sister, actress Mackenzie Phillips, was a bridesmaid. Also on hand were Chynna's Wilson Phillips band mates, Wendy and talkmeister Carnie Wilson, who had witnessed the couple's first meeting, on a plane in 1991. "We could see Billy sticking his head into the aisle to watch her," recalls Carnie. "I said, 'Honey, this is it!' "

For the bride, this Shue was a perfect fit: Melrose Place *star Andrew Shue, 28, did the princely thing when he swept his Cinderella (and former agent) Jennifer Hageney, 31, off her feet. After three years and two broken engagements, Melissa Gilbert, 30, who played Laura Ingalls on* Little House on the Prairie, *and* Babylon 5's *Bruce Boxleitner, 44, finally succumbed to fate. The bride's sister, Sara* (Roseanne) *Gilbert, was maid of honor at a ceremony Melissa strategically arranged to occur on New Year's Day. "Now, she says, "Bruce can't forget our anniversary."*

His body all but stilled by motor neuron disease, Stephen Hawking, 53, the physicist and author of the best-selling A Brief History of Time, *wed his nurse Elaine Mason, 45. The physicist left his first wife, Jane, after she devoted 25 years to his care and, despite his illness, conceived three children with him.*

Today *show weatherman Al Roker, 41, felt himself getting a bit misty-eyed as he watched his bride, 20/20 correspondent Deborah Roberts, 34, walk down the aisle. "I can't puddle," Roker scolded himself. He didn't.* Baywatch *star Pamela Anderson, 27, wore a bikini when she wound up a five-day fling in Cancun, Mexico, by marrying rocker (and Heather Locklear's ex) Tommy Lee, 32. Explains Pamela: "It was instant mind-blowing animal attraction."*

Friends star *Lisa Kudrow*, 31, and French ad executive *Michel Stern*, 37, wrote their own vows for their Malibu do. Notes Kudrow: "They had to be short because we said them in French and English.

Revlon tycoon *Ron Perelman*, 52, and Democratic political activist *Patricia Duff*, 40.

Professional golfer *John Daly*, 28, and former model *Paulette Dean*, 23.

Former Nixon aide and convicted Watergate conspirator *John Ehrlichman*, 69, and Atlanta restaurateur *Karen Hilliard*.

Neo-folkie *Suzanne Vega*, 35, and music producer *Mitchell Froom*, 31.

Wild at heart or true romance? Screen stars *Nicolas Cage*, 31, and *Patricia Arquette*, 27.

Rapper-actor *Tupac Shakur*, 23, and *Keisha Morris*, at the Clinton Correctional Facility in Dannemora, New York. Shakur, found guilty in December 1994 of sexually abusing a fan, was sentenced to 4½ years.

Rapper *LL Cool J* (James Smith), 25, and *Simone Johnson*, the mother of his two kids.

Massachusetts Democratic Sen. *John Kerry*, 51, and *Teresa Heinz*, 56, widow of Republican Sen. H. John Heinz of Pennsylvania, who died in a plane crash in 1991. She is vice chairwoman of the Environmental Defense Fund.

Pride & Joy's *Julie Warner*, 30, and *Camp Nowhere* writer-director *Jonathan Prince*, 36.

Model *Stephanie Seymour*, 26, and millionaire *Interview* magazine owner *Peter Brant*, 48.

Musician *Ike Turner*, 63, Tina's ex, and dancer-singer *Jeanette Bazzell*, 32.

Actor *Tom Arnold*, 36, Roseanne's ex, and *Julie Champnella*, 22, a former student at Eastern Michigan University.

Christie Hefner, 42, Hugh's daughter and the current Playboy CEO, and lawyer *Bill Marovitz*, 50. Sex therapist Ruth Westheimer attended the wedding and said: "The way they looked at each other and touched, I know they don't need me."

Assistant Secretary of State *Richard Holbrooke*, 54, Clinton's troubleshooter in Bosnia and Diane Sawyer's former boyfriend, and author *Kati Marton*, 46, Peter Jennings's ex.

Marriage was never a piece of cake for Roseanne, 42, who nevertheless went back for thirds with her ex-bodyguard Ben Thomas, 28. Trouble—and Tonya—behind her, skater Nancy Kerrigan, 25, finally got her gold when she hitched up with her agent, Jerry Solomon, 41. Aging teen idol Shaun Cassidy, 36, still knows how to make a girl quiver. "My heart jumps every time I see him," says Susan Diol, 30, who read for the part of Cassidy's wife in a proposed Partridge Family TV *movie, then snagged the role in real life.*

WEDDINGS 1995

Wings's *Steven Weber*, 34, and MTV's L.A. bureau chief, *Juliette Hohnen*, 30.

NYPD Blue actress *Gail O'Grady*, 32, and her manager *Steven Fenton*, 28.

Ukulele-strumming singer *Tiny Tim*, 72, and Harvard-educated *Susan Gardner*, 39.

Species star *Natasha Henstridge*, 21, and *Damian Chapa*, 32, of *Bound by Honor*.

Singer *Gladys Knight*, 51, and motivational speaker *Les Brown*, 50.

Palm Beach lady of letters *Roxanne Pulitzer*, 44, and businessman *Harold Dude*, 51. Pulitzer's marriage to her third husband, socialite John Haggin Jr., lasted 57 days.

Actress *Amy Brenneman*, 31, and *Brad Silberling*, 32, who directed her in *Casper*.

ABC News correspondent *John Hockenberry*, 39, and ABC News producer *Alison Craiglow*, 28.

Actress *Meg Tilly*, 35, and United Artists studio president *John Calley*, 65.

There was something borrowed (a handkerchief) but nothing blue when comedian Martin Lawrence, 29, degartered his bride, Patricia Southall, 24, a former Miss Virginia. Having gone through drug rehab, Beach Boys founder Brian Wilson, 52, had fun, fun, fun when he wed Melinda Ledbetter, 47. Though former General Hospital *hunk Tristan Rogers, 48, and Teresa Parkinson, 31, didn't rush to the altar (their daughter Sara, 2, was the flower girl), the ceremony was quick. Says Rogers: "It was, 'I do, we do, okay, let's go.'"*

WEDDINGS 1995

The Rev. and Mrs. Sun Myung Moon, the Unification Church heads who in 1992 married 30,000 couples at once, blessed the arranged unions of their son *Kwon-Jin*, 20, to *Hwa-Yun Chun*, and their daughter *Sun-Jin*, 19, to *In-Sup Park*, 24. "In my church, marriage is like a box of chocolates," says Moon son-in-law In-Sup. "You never know what you're gonna get!"

Extra anchor *Arthel Neville*, 32, and Carolina Panther running back *Derrick Lassic*, 25.

Former *Petticoat Junction* star *Meredith MacRae*, 48, and office-supply company president *Philip Neal*, 54.

Actress *Meredith Baxter*, 48, and *Michael Blodgett*, 56, screenwriter of *Turner and Hooch*. The family affair included Baxter's five children from her two previous marriages, and Blodgett's three children.

Ike's granddaughter *Susan Eisenhower*, 43, and *Roald Sagdeev*, 62, the former head of the Soviet space program. They met at a Soviet-American conference in 1987, which she attended as president of the Eisenhower World Affairs Institute, and courted with coded telexed love notes.

The Heidi Fleiss flap behind him (he'd been a $50,000 client of the Hollywood Madam), Charlie Sheen, 30, wed model Donna Peele, 25. Bruce Springsteen and Billy Joel were among the guests when Eagles legend Don Henley, 47, tied the knot with model Sharon Summerall, 33. And Prince Rainier of Monaco finally gave his blessing to the union of Princess Stephanie, 30, and bodyguard Daniel Ducruet, 31, the father of her two toddlers.

The Rev. Jesse Jackson presided at the nuptials of Hangin' with Mr. Cooper's *Holly Robinson, 30,* and Philadelphia Eagle quarterback *Rodney Peete, 29.* Thirteen years after meeting on a dance floor, NYPD Blue's *Dennis Franz, 50,* partnered with businesswoman *Joanie Zeck, 47.* The TV tough guy even picked out the flowers for the occasion.

Bill and Hillary Clinton helped their fellow Arkansan *Mary Steenburgen, 42,* celebrate her marriage to *Ted Danson, 47,* at Martha's Vineyard. The President recalled pulling Danson aside at a White House dinner and growled, "Listen I love this girl. Better do right by her."

WEDDINGS 1995

L.A. Raiders defensive end *Anthony Smith,* 27, and *Denise Matthews,* 36, a Prince protégé formerly known as Vanity.

Princess Elena of Spain, 31, and banker *Jaime de Marichalar,* 31. Members of 38 royal families were invited to Spain's first royal wedding since 1906.

Queen Elizabeth, Prince Charles and King Hussein were among the royals gathered in London for the nuptials of exiled *Crown Prince Pavlos* of Greece, 28, and American heiress *Marie-Chantal Miller,* 26, daughter of Robert W. Miller, 62, cofounder of Duty Free Shoppers Ltd.

Julie Krone, 32, the world's top female jockey, and TV sports producer *Matthew Muzikar,* 26. Getting to church on time came down to a photo finish for Krone, who rode in six races in Saratoga on her wedding day.

The Donald's ex, *Ivana Trump,* 46, and her Roman Romeo, Italian businessman *Riccardo Mazzucchelli,* 52. "I don't depend on a man to survive," says Ivana, who is worth an estimated $35 million. "But I like to have a man to fuss around with."

Van Halen band member *Sammy Hagar,* 46, and model *Kari Karte.*

95

SPECIAL DELIVERY

Deidre Hall, 47, was still wearing satanic makeup from her role as a demonically possessed shrink on *Days of Our Lives*, when she raced to join her husband, TV producer Steve Sohmer, 53, who was waiting with an overnight bag. Nine hours later, their second son, Tully, arrived, as Hall says, "in the sweetest and gentlest way"—but hardly the most conventional. For it wasn't Hall giving birth but rather a surrogate mom who two years earlier had carried the couple's first child, David Atticus. "We're older parents," explains Hall. "We knew we wouldn't be here all of David's life and we wanted to give him a sibling." So far, these uniquely conceived brothers seem to be bonding nicely. "David," says Hall, "wants the baby to sleep in *his* room."

After years of feudin', the Judds called a truce to welcome baby Elijah (left, with his ma, Wynonna, 30, and pa, Arch Kelley III, 43). The day of the birth, grandma Naomi, Wynonna's old singing partner, tried to take over the show. "She was putting up the screen so nobody could see me," says Wynonna, "as if I care what people see! I said, 'You will never quit, will you?' " Liam Neeson, 43, took a break from a film about the IRA when his wife, Natasha Richardson, 32, gave birth to an Irish laddie: Michéal.

Actor-director and hyper sports fan Spike Lee, 37, believes his wife, Tonya Lewis, 33, hit one out of the park when she named their daughter Satchel, evoking the memory of the legendary pitcher Satchel Paige. Gymnast Mary Lou Retton, 27, the golden girl of the 1984 Olympics, teamed with her husband, Shannon Kelley, 29, to deliver another perfect 10 in 1995: Shayla Rae Kelley. Yasser, that's his baby. Suha Arafat, 32, wife of PLO leader Yasser Arafat, 65, showed off their firstborn, Zahwa, in Paris before taking her to Gaza, where a new Palestinian amusement park had already been named in her honor. Zahwa means pride in Arabic.

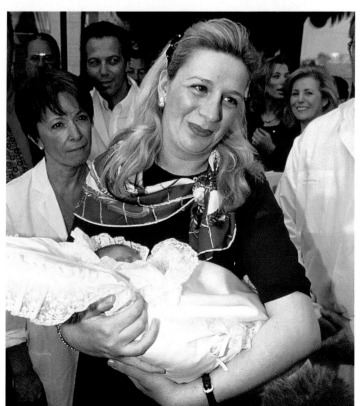

BIRTHS 1995

Actor *Daniel Day-Lewis*, 38, and actress *Isabelle Adjani*, 39; a son.

Rocker *Bob Seger*, 50, and wife *Nita*, 31; daughter Samantha Char.

Rocker *John Mellencamp*, 43, and model *Elaine Irwin*, 25; son Speck Wildhorse.

Comic *David Brenner*, 50, and artist *Elizabeth Bryan Slater*, 33; son Slade Lucas Moby.

Mötley Crüe bassist *Nikki Sixx*, 36, and his wife, *Brandi*, 26, an ex-model; son Decker Nilsson.

Christie Brinkley, 41, and real estate developer *Rick Taubman*, 46; son Jack Paris, five months after they split.

Comedian and now single mom *Rosie O'Donnell*, 33; son Parker Jaren, by adoption.

Actor *Dudley Moore*, 60, and wife, *Nicole Rothschild*, 31; son Nicholas Anthony.

Mad About You's *Paul Reiser*, 39, and his psychotherapist wife, *Paula*, 32; son Ezra Samuel.

Rocker *Eddie Money*, 46, and wife *Laurie*, 30; son Matthew Julian.

Stanley Burrell, 32, better known as rapper *M.C. Hammer*, and wife, *Stephanie*, 28; son Stanley Kirk, Jr.

Big-screen kickboxer *Jean-Claude Van Damme,* 35, and his fourth wife *Darcy LaPier,* 30; son Nicolas.

Actor *Chazz Palminteri*, 44, and actress *Gianna Renaudo*, 29; son Dante Lorenzo.

Hollywood kids paraded their star genes in '95. Lorraine Nicholson, 5, daughter of Wolf *man Jack, displayed a flair for evening wear at a stage production of* Beauty and the Beast. *Jamie Lee Curtis's daughter Annie, 9, and mom Janet Leigh cheered Curtis at a screening of* The Heidi Chronicles. *And Kevin Costner made a splash bringing his brood (from left, Lily, 9, Joe, 7, and Annie, 11, to the premiere of* Waterworld.

BIRTHS 1995

Braveheart's Sophie Marceau, 28, and Polish director *Andrzej Zulawski,* 52; son Vincent.

U2 drummer *Larry Mullen Jr.,* 34, and girlfriend *Anne Acheson,* 32; son Aaron Elvis.

Supergirl's Helen Slater, 31, and filmmaker *Bob Watzke,* 35; daughter Hannah Nika.

Film critic *Gene Siskel,* 49, and former TV producer *Marlene Iglitzen,* 42; son Will Nathaniel.

Actor *Tony Goldwyn,* 34, and production designer *Jane Musky,* 40; daughter Tess Frances.

Singer-actress *Andrea Marcovicci,* 46, and actor *Daniel Reichert,* 33; daughter Alice Wolfe.

The Love Boat's Jill Whelan, and businessman *Brad St. John,* 33; son Harrison Robert.

Actor *James Caan,* 55, and wife *Linda,* 39; son James Arthur.

Former Olympic decathlon champ *Bruce Jenner,* 46, and wife *Kris,* 38; daughter Kendall Nicole.

Former NBA superstar *Earvin "Magic" Johnson,* 36, and wife *Cookie,* 35; daughter Elisa, by adoption.

Talk show host *Marilu Henner,* 43, and director *Robert Lieberman,* 47; son Joseph Marlon.

Jane Seymour, 44, of *Dr. Quinn, Medicine Woman,* and actor-director *James Keach,* 48; twin sons, John Stacy and Kristopher Steven.

Film director *Oliver Stone ,* 49, and model *Chong Son Chong,* 36; daughter Tara.

Showing they know how to get down with the younger set, actress Alfre Woodard and her husband, writer Roderick Spencer, sparkled with their own beauties—Mavis, 3, and Duncan, 16 months, at the L.A. opening of Beauty and the Beast. *At the Fire and Ice Ball to benefit the Revlon/UCLA Women's Cancer Research Program in L.A. Cher came with her son Elijah Blue, 18, who showed the smart 'do (or don't) among the student-and-sometime-musician set.* General Hospital's *Kristina Malandro and husband Jack Wagner, her former costar and suds stud before he moved to* Melrose Place, *cozied up to their kids Peter, 5, and Harrison, 10 months, at Nickelodeon's Big Help-a-Thon in L.A., where kids pledge to devote a few hours to community service.*

"They look so happy together," says matchmaker Lauri Keller of her birth parents, Larry Kellem and Barbara Colvin.

REKINDLING OLD FIRES

For three decades, the only time Lauri Keller had been with both of her biological parents was the day she was born. On October 28, 1963, at George Washington University Hospital in Washington, D.C., Barbara Colvin, then 20, gave birth to a daughter; the father, her college boyfriend Larry Kellem, 24, was at her side. But after an agonizing month, Colvin had decided to give the infant up for adoption and go on with her life—apart from Kellem.

Though Lauri, now a San Diego-based marketing consultant, had always been curious about her birth parents, it was not until 1991 that she got up the courage to contact the original adoption agency to try to find them. Coincidentally, Colvin too had just phoned the agency after going through some old belongings and finding a letter postmarked December 1963, informing her that the baby she had named Anya had been adopted. Colvin, now an antiques store owner in Billerica, Massachusetts, subsequently tracked down Kellem, who owns a lawn-sprinkler business in nearby Upton, and told him that she wanted to find their child. Kellem agreed, saying: "If my daughter wanted to meet me, I would do it."

In February 1993, Lauri was reunited with her mother in San Diego and a few months later traveled east to meet her father. Then, eager to see the two together, Lauri arranged for all three to meet at a Boston restaurant. As she watched Kellem, the divorced father of a teenage son, and Colvin, a mother of two other grown kids who was in a troubled second marriage, she sensed they were still in love. After Colvin got divorced in 1994, Keller encouraged her parents to date. They did. And a year later she served as bridesmaid when Barbara, now 52, wed Kellem, 56. "This whole thing has been like a dream," says Lauri. "I believe in my heart that they belong together. The feelings were there. I just sort of stoked the flame."

DADDY MEANEST

Marilyn Kane could not bear even to look at her ex-husband Jeffrey Nichols as he took the stand and begged a judge for compassion. His business had collapsed, he insisted—there was only $5 left in a checking account. He had just buried his second wife, who had died quickly after being diagnosed with lung cancer. New York State Supreme Court Justice Phyllis Gangel-Jacob listened intently but was unmoved. For the court, the issue was, simply, $580,000. That was the amount of child support Nichols owed Kane, and his was the largest prosecution ever under a new federal law designed to guarantee that children get money to which they are entitled. If Nichols did not have the cash, ruled Gangel-Jacob, he would have to get it. She ordered him jailed until he came up with at least $68,000.

So ended the legal pursuit of America's most notorious deadbeat dad, Nichols, 47, who until a few weeks before had been living the good life of a precious-metals consultant in his $500,000 home in Charlotte, Vermont. Kane, 47, was triumphant. "My children have been carrying Mr. Nichols's shame for years," she said. "It's time we gave that shame back to Mr. Nichols." Since his 1990 divorce from Marilyn, who married insurance broker David Kane the same year, Nichols had done everything in his power—including moving from New York to Ontario to Florida to Vermont—to avoid his $9,000-a-month child-support payments. At one point he even claimed he was not the father of Joshua, now 22, Julie, 20, and Joseph, 15. "I don't blame anybody but myself," Nichols testified. "I have a great deal of guilt." No one would disagree. Even if he eventually manages to pay his debt, he still faces prosecution for allegedly abandoning his wife and children, charges that carry up to a six-month jail term.

If Nichols is not the typical deadbeat father—most are out of work and poor themselves—then neither is Kane, a former schoolteacher, the typical mother left in the lurch. Unlike many abandoned women, she had the means, education and relentless determination to see Nichols brought to justice. "I know that many women can't afford to go after their husbands," she said. "I'm doing this for them."

"It makes you sick," says Kane of the failure of her now jailed ex, Nichols, to pay child support. "He got what he deserved." Their son Josh (above left, with siblings Julie and Joseph) agrees. "It was very hurtful when he wrote us off."

BRAWL IN THE FAMILY

As he entered the awkward age of adolescence, Macaulay Culkin, 15, discovered that home is where the heartache is. Though he had earned more than $50 million since his 1990 debut in *Home Alone*, his last three films—*Getting Even with Dad*, *The Pagemaster* and *Richie Rich*—were all box office disappointments. Meanwhile, Christopher "Kit" Culkin, 51, a former child actor himself who many had come to view as the stage father from hell, was locked in legal combat with his common-law wife, Patricia Brentrup, 41. Patty petitioned a Manhattan court to give her custody of their six minor children and the right to manage their careers. "[Culkin] and I have been separated in the past due to his excessive drinking, physical abuse and unfaithful behavior," Brentrup said in court papers. Kit Culkin, in his reply, called her statement "fabrications, half-truths and outright lies."

Mac had taken a breather from movie work in 1995 and went from cute cherub to teen slacker. He dyed his hair a punkish magenta for a while, then went back to blond. He apparently managed to pay a visit to his old pal Michael Jackson at his Neverland ranch, but otherwise stayed home most of the summer with his siblings Shane, 19, and Dakota, 17, while their parents and the younger kids—Quinn, 10, Christian, 8, and Rory, 6, set up divided camp near the Montana set where Kieran, 12, was filming *Amanda*. Joining the clan briefly in Montana, Mac was present one night when police answered a 911 call from the childrens' nanny during a family squabble.

Returning to Manhattan's Professional Children's school in the fall, Mac waited for the custody war to play itself out in court. With producers no longer burning up the lines with new projects, the most famous child actor since Shirley Temple had other outlets. "All he really wants to do," says his dad's lawyer, "is play basketball."

"He used to be more boisterous," says a friend of the former Home Alone *star, Macauley Culkin, hanging out with pals in New York City.*

THE WIDOW WORE WHITE

In June 1994, *Playboy* model and *Naked Gun 33 1/3: The Final Insult* actress Anna Nicole Smith, then 27, married Houston oil tycoon J. Howard Marshall II, 89. Cynics speculated that Smith had wed the wheelchair-bound zillionaire for reasons other than romance. Protested the hurt bride: "I know people think I married Howard for his money. But it's not true." Fast forward one year, when Marshall died of pneumonia. Not only did the question of what would happen to his fortune, estimated at more than $500 million, acquire a new urgency but there was also the more immediate concern of who should arrange the funeral.

Marshall's son, Pierce, 54, who was granted power of attorney over his father's money shortly after the marriage, had planned a dignified, private memorial service. Before that could take place, however, Smith staged a memorable service of her own. Two teddy bears sat by Marshall's casket, and guests were treated to the sight of Smith in a white gown with its decolletage at half-mast. Weeping, she warbled, "Wind Beneath My Wings," while her tiny black dog wandered the aisles. Pierce went ahead with a more solemn ceremony a week later, which Smith skipped. But the grieving widow did show up a day later at a court hearing wearing a modest black dress and minimal makeup. The docket concerned Marshall's remains: Pierce had planned to have his father cremated; Smith objected.

What seemed really at issue was which Marshall heir would gain the legal upper hand for control of his millions. The first skirmish ended in an arrangement: Marshall would be cremated—with his ashes divided between the two sides. "I think it's fair," Smith said. "I'm glad it's over." But with the money not yet divvied up, the battle had only just begun.

At her husband's funeral, Smith donned a veil: the same one she wore for their wedding 14 months before.

BEFORE
HER TIME

A friend's bullet cut short the life of beloved Tex-Mex music queen **SELENA**— *one of the youngest luminaries we mourned in '95*

Onstage, Selena was smoldering, flirtatious and passionate, yet she once turned down a role in a Mexican soap opera because it called for a kissing scene. She was known as the Madonna of Tejano music, yet she was guided always by tradition and family. By the time she was 23, her music had made her wealthy, yet she and her husband, Chris Pérez, still lived next door to her parents in the modest Molina neighborhood of Corpus Christi, Texas. "Selena was from the barrio," a disc jockey told mourners at a memorial service the day after her death. "She still ate tortillas and frijoles."

She blazed and shimmered in the spotlight, but it was the fact that Selena was happily, proudly *del pueblo*—"of the people"—that forged a powerful, personal bond between her and her audience. In the saddest of ironies, it was apparently her trust in a fan—and a friend—that cut short a life poised on the brink of even greater success and celebrity. Selena had gone to a room in the Days Inn motel in Corpus Christi to confront the former president of her fan club, Yolanda Saldívar, 34. Saldívar, suspected by Selena and her family of embezzling funds, was on the verge of being fired, and she knew it. Soon after Selena arrived, Saldívar shot her once in the back with a .38-caliber revolver.

The tragedy sped Selena's inevitable breakthrough into the Anglo market, and her posthumous album *Dreaming of You* sold 331,000 copies in its first week. She was a treasure awaiting discovery. When she died, 50,000 people came together at a service in Corpus Christi to weep in her memory. "We all cried in my family, too," a young girl wrote to Selena's parents. "She lives in all of our hearts and in her music."

"When I had to say goodbye to her at the funeral, I was going crazy," says Selena's guitarist husband, Chris Pérez, 25 (with her at a charity softball game, far left, top, in San Antonio in 1993). "I wanted to crawl into the coffin and put my arms around her and go to sleep next to her and have them close the lid and bury me with her." At the 1995 Tejano Music Awards in San Antonio, Selena posed with Los Caporals and was named Female Entertainer of the Year for the eighth consecutive time. At the Grammys in March, the ever more mainstream star schmoozed with Bonnie Raitt and wore a favorite gown that she would be buried in four weeks later. Below, at Hollywood's Sunset and Vine, fans gathered outside a radio station to mourn their fallen favorite. "Everyone feels so bad," said one station employee. "Selena means everything."

GEORGE KIRBY

George Kirby described himself as "the first black stand-up comedian—before me, they were buck and wing." He began his career in Las Vegas in the '40s, when black entertainers were not allowed to gamble or stay at the hotels where they performed. On the club circuit and as a frequent guest on television variety shows, Kirby built up a repertoire of more than 100 uncanny impersonations, ranging from Walter Brennan and Humphrey Bogart to Pearl Bailey and Sarah Vaughan. He also developed a nasty drug habit and spent 3½ years in prison after getting busted in 1977 for selling cocaine and heroin to a federal undercover agent. Stricken with Parkinson's disease, Kirby had been paralyzed for several months before his death at age 71.

BOBBY RIGGS

In 1939, as a 21-year-old upstart from Los Angeles, he took Wimbledon by storm, winning the singles, doubles and mixed doubles in his first try—establishing a record that has yet to be broken. But Bobby Riggs earned greater reknown among later generations as a showboating male chauvinist. Before a much ballyhooed "Battle of the Sexes" match in 1973 with women's tennis champion Billie Jean King, Riggs, then 55, declared, "When I get through with Billie she might just go home and start raising a family. That's where women should be, barefoot and pregnant." Riggs was stunned when King beat him 6–4, 6–3, 6–3 in front of 50 million TV viewers, but he cheerfully carried home $1.5 million in prize money. According to King, who remained a friend of the amiable sports-world hustler until his death at 77 from prostate cancer, the match "helped put women's tennis on the map."

ELIZABETH MONTGOMERY

She was an enchantress who cast a spell over an entire generation of TV viewers in *Bewitched*. In her signature role as Samantha Stephens, a blithe, blonde witch determined to be the perfect wife to a sputteringly flustered ad man, Elizabeth Montgomery worked her magic with a twitch of her nose.

The daughter of movie star Robert Montgomery and stage actress Elizabeth Allen, Montgomery kept her personal life far from the limelight. "She was shy," says her fourth husband, actor Robert Foxworth, 53. In the moments before her death at age 62 from colon cancer, Foxworth honored her request for privacy by waiting in another room with her three children, aged 25 to 30, from her third marriage (to *Bewitched* producer William Asher).

After an eight-year run on *Bewitched* ended in 1972, Montgomery became the doyenne of TV movies, playing everyone from Lizzie Borden to Belle Starr. She was a star without a star attitude, says Miami crime reporter Edna Buchanan, whom Montgomery portrayed in *The Corpse Had a Familiar Face* (1992) and *Deadline for Murder*, completed eight weeks before her death. One night they were dining together, Buchanan remembers, and everyone from the busboy to the maitre d' greeted Montgomery and asked her how she was doing. She in turn asked all of them about their friends and families. "Elizabeth just acted like a terrific, friendly, wonderful, buoyant person," says Buchanan. The magic didn't end with Samantha.

GOODBYES 1995

Actor *Don Brockett*, 65, who had been rolling out dough and whipping up entrées as Chef Brockett on TV's *Mister Rogers' Neighborhood* since 1967; of a heart attack.

Counterculture clothing designer *Holly Harp*, 55, who dressed rock icons Janis Joplin and Grace Slick in tie-dye and fringe; of cancer.

Actress *Katherine DeMille Quinn*, 83, the first wife of movie star Anthony Quinn and the adopted daughter of biblical-epic director Cecil B. DeMille; of Alzheimer's disease.

Satirist *Terry Southern*, 71, who cowrote the screenplays for *Dr. Strangelove* and *Easy Rider*, and 1964's best-seller *Candy*; of respiratory failure.

Director *Frank Perry*, 65, whose films included *David and Lisa* (1962), *Diary of a Mad Housewife* (1970), *Mommie Dearest* (1981) and *Compromising Positions* (1985); of prostate cancer.

Political and social activist *Maggie Kuhn*, 89, who led the fight against age discrimination by helping to found the Gray Panthers in 1970; of cardiopulmonary arrest.

Tough-guy character actor *Harry Guardino*, 69, who appeared in more than 30 films, including *Houseboat* (1958) and *Dirty Harry* (1971) and in recent years was a frequent guest star on CBS's *Murder, She Wrote*; of lung cancer.

WARREN BURGER

Former Chief Justice Warren Burger, who died of heart failure at 87, presided over the Supreme Court for 17 years, longer than anyone else this century. Appointed by President Richard Nixon in 1969, Burger later spoke for a unanimous court when he ordered Nixon to hand over his Watergate tapes. Despite Burger's own conservative leanings, the court during his tenure legalized abortion and upheld affirmative action. And even after he stepped down as the nation's 15th chief justice, the white-haired Burger could be often be seen riding around D.C. in the back of a stretch limousine whose license plate read: "CJ 15."

ROBERT O'DONNELL

When Jessica McClure, not yet 2 years old, tumbled down an old well in Midland, Texas, in October 1987, Robert O'Donnell was the paramedic who squirmed down the dangerously narrow rescue shaft and edged her, inch by inch, back to safety. "I've saved other people's lives before," O'Donnell said, "but there'll never be nothing like this again."

Nearly eight years later, O'Donnell, 37, added a tragic postscript to the Baby Jessica story that had made him a national hero. Hours after his mother noticed a shotgun missing from her ranch, police found O'Donnell slumped in his new Ford pickup, a victim of suicide. Friends say he never recovered from the quicksilver fame the rescue brought him. His marriage subsequently ended in divorce, and his career at the Midland Fire Department collapsed amid allegations of prescription-drug abuse. "Once the adrenaline [subsides], you go into a major depression," says police Sgt. Andy Glasscock, another of Jessica's rescuers. "Robert never came out of it. We saved a little girl, but we've all lost a friend."

LANA TURNER

She is preserved in memory as she was on celluloid: a luminous sex goddess whose looks could melt a monk's resolve. The Sweater Girl, they called her. Lana Turner made 54 films, playing every variety of girl—good, bad, sometimes heartless. But despite her portrayal of the icy adulteress in 1946's *The Postman Always Rings Twice*, "she was the opposite of her hard-boiled image," says Teri Garr, who in 1980 worked with Turner on her last film, the never-released *Witches' Brew*. "She was very sweet; a gracious, genteel woman."

Her 74 years were dogged, however, with sadness and pain. She had seven failed marriages, three miscarriages, two abortions and a suicide attempt. More vividly remembered than any of her movies, perhaps, is the great scandal in which she played a leading role. In 1958, the actress's 14-year-old daughter, Cheryl, fatally stabbed Turner's gangster boyfriend, Johnny Stompanato, in their Beverly Hills home.

Even after she was diagnosed with throat cancer in 1992, Turner insisted that a hairdresser visit her twice a week. On her birthday two years ago she told friends—in a hoarse whisper—that she was "completely recovered." It was a final, fitting performance from the star. For Lana Turner, in the words of her former secretary Taylor Pero, lived by only three precepts: "Image before truth, facade rather than fact, and pride over all."

Novelist and screenwriter *Calder Willingham*, 72, author of *End as a Man* and Oscar nominee with cowriter Buck Henry for the screenplay of 1967's *The Graduate*; of lung cancer.

Writer *Sir Stephen Spender*, 86, one of the so-called Oxford poets of the 1930s, who, moved by impending war and declining social conditions, merged literature and radical politics; of natural causes.

British playwright and screenwriter *Robert Bolt*, 70, who wrote such classic films as *Lawrence of Arabia* (1962), *Doctor Zhivago* (1965), *A Man for All Seasons* (1966), which was based on his original play, and *Ryan's Daughter* (1970); of undisclosed causes.

Singer *Melvin Franklin*, 52, one of five original members of the Temptations, whose bass voice anchored the harmonies for such Motown hits as "My Girl" and "The Way You Do the Things You Do"; of heart failure.

Playwright and actor *Michael V. Gazzo*, 71, who wrote Broadway's *A Hatful of Rain* and played Mafia lieutenant Frank Pentangeli in *The Godfather, Part II* (1974); of a stroke.

British director *Jack Clayton*, 73, whose films included *Room at the Top* (1959) and *The Great Gatsby* (1974); of heart and liver problems.

WOLFMAN JACK

Brooklynite Robert Weston Smith first rumbled onto nationwide radio waves as Wolfman Jack in 1964 over a pirate Mexican station whose 250,000-watt signal—illegal under U.S. laws—beamed his high-pitched howl across the border and turned him into a cult hero. After appearing as himself in the 1973 film *American Graffiti*, he hosted TV's *Midnight Special*. When he died of a heart attack at his Belvidere, North Carolina, home, he was still broadcasting an oldies show to 80 stations nationally. His last howl came at age 57.

DR. JONAS SALK

The call came about 12 years ago, as AIDS was making its terrible presence felt. "I remember my secretary saying, 'Jonas Salk is on the phone,' " recalls Dr. Anthony Fauci, director of the National Institute of Allergy and Infectious Diseases at the National Institutes of Health in Bethesda, Maryland. "I thought she was kidding. But I got on the phone, and he started asking me questions about immunology." Dr. Jonas Salk was determined to defeat the new scourge. He fell short, but until his death of heart failure at age 80, he was still at work on an AIDS vaccine.

It was the same determination that had led Salk to one of the century's most celebrated medical breakthroughs: the virtual eradication of polio. In 1952 nearly 58,000 cases were reported in the United States, more than 3,000 of them fatal. As public hysteria grew, Salk committed himself to the then-radical notion that an effective virus could be made from killed—as opposed to live but neutralized—viruses. And after 1969, the disease almost vanished in America.

Salk and his second wife, Françoise Gilot, Pablo Picasso's former mistress and mother of Claude and Paloma Picasso, were benefactors to several museums. But fame hardly seemed to interest him. Says Wylie Vale, faculty chairman of the Salk Institute for Biological Studies in La Jolla, California : "He would tell kids to live their dreams; that before anything was a reality, it was a dream."

YITZHAK RABIN

It is an irony of history that the most lasting image of Yitzhak Rabin—the Israeli prime minister who fell to an assassin's bullets at age 73—may be his 1993 White House handclasp with Palestinian leader Yasser Arafat. The more private Rabin was a rough-edged career soldier with no taste for the glad-handing that came with high office. He smoked four packs of cigarettes a day, lighting each new one with the butt of the last. His sense of humor was as dry as the Judean desert, and he spoke an unrefined Hebrew peppered with crude street slang. All of that caused many of his people to love him. He was one of them.

His taciturn toughness came from growing up as a Jew in the embattled atmosphere of prewar Palestine. The son of Russian immigrants, Rabin joined the Haganah, the militia precursor to Israel's army, during World War II. He played a key role in the 1948 battle for independence and was the chief of staff who orchestrated Israel's sweeping victory in 1967's Six Day War. After his stunning success on the battlefield, Rabin was made ambassador to the United States in 1967. Seven years later he became briefly prime minister, the first sabra, or native-born Israeli, to rise to the post. In 1992 Rabin was voted into office again, promising that his Labor party would lead the way toward peace with the Palestinians and the surrounding Arab nations. His killer, tragically, was a Jew, a zealot from the antipeace movement.

To the end, Rabin remained spartan and unpretentious. When he took his first foreign post, a colleague had to tie his necktie, and in his eulogy, President Clinton recalled Rabin's showing up for a White House black-tie event without the black tie. He borrowed one, "and I was privileged to straighten it for him," said Clinton. "It is a moment I will cherish as long as I live."

GOODBYES 1995

Character actress *Mary Wickes*, 85, a vet of 50 films and TV shows, last seen in *Little Women*; of complications following surgery.

Stand-up comedian *Slappy White*, 74, a regular on the 1970's series *Sanford and Son*; of a heart attack.

Writer *Henry Roth*, 89, whose 1934 novel *Call It Sleep* documented the struggle of immigrants in New York City.

Maxene Andrews, 79, of the singing Andrews Sisters, who found fame in the '30s and '40s with hits like "Don't Sit Under the Apple Tree"; of a heart attack.

Astrologer *Patric Walker*, 64, who dispensed heavenly advice to millions of newspaper readers worldwide; after a severe case of salmonella.

Extroverted baseball umpire *Ron Luciano*, 57, who called runners out by cocking his fingers, pistol-like, and gunning them down; by his own hand, letting his car engine idle in a closed garage.

Evelyn Lincoln, 85, John F. Kennedy's devoted secretary from 1953, his first year in the U.S. Senate, until his assassination 10 years later; of complications after cancer surgery.

Blind Melon lead singer *Shannon Hoon*, 28; of an apparent drug overdose.

Longtime ABC News correspondent *John Scali*, 77, whose behind-the-scenes negotiations with the Soviets in 1963 helped resolve the Cuban missile crisis; of heart failure.

EVA GABOR

She was both ditsy and dignified in her most memorable role as a down-on-the-farm socialite on TV's 1965–71 hit series *Green Acres*. A Hungarian native, Eva Gabor immigrated to the U.S. in 1939 (later followed by big sisters Zsa Zsa and Magda) in hopes of becoming a movie star. She worked her way into secondary roles in *My Man Godfrey* (1957), *Gigi* (1958) and other films, but it was her image as a chatty, much-wed (five times) glamor queen and companion of entertainer-casino magnate Merv Griffin that kept her busy on talk shows and propelled her into prime time. "We Gabors are supposed to do nothing but take bubble baths and drip with jewels," observed the actress, before her death of pneumonia at 74. "But I've worked like a demon. I didn't have time to sit in bubbles."

GEORGE ABBOTT

He was Mr. Broadway. For more than seven decades, George Abbott, who lived to 107, towered over the Great White Way as playwright, director, actor and producer. Renowned for his snappy pacing, he was a peerless script doctor—legend has it he told director Hal Prince how to chop an act of the classic *Cabaret* (1966). His many honors—a shared Pulitzer with Jerome Weidman for the book of 1959's *Fiorello!* and Tonys for 1954's *Pajama Game*, 1955's *Damn Yankees* and 1962's *A Funny Thing Happened on the Way to the Forum*—were capped by a special Distinguished Career Achievement Tony in 1976 and a Kennedy Center award in 1982. "Everybody on Broadway today has been influenced by George Abbott," says Gwen Verdon, who was the lead in *Damn Yankees* 42 years ago.

Abbott enjoyed golfing and dancing into his 100s with his third wife, Joy Valderrama, a furrier more than 40 years his junior. When asked the secret of his longevity, Abbott, whose final work was helping reshape the 1994 revival of *Damn Yankees*, advised simply, "Have fun. And go home when you're tired."

KRISSY TAYLOR

It had been a long evening for Krissy Taylor, 17. The cover girl—and little sister of 20-year-old supermodel Niki Taylor—had spent the night of July 1 with Niki watching the Hooters football team play the Connecticut Coyotes in Miami. Back home in Pembroke Pines by midnight, Krissy kissed her mother, Barbara, goodnight around 2:30 a.m. Two hours later, Niki, who had gone out after the game with husband Matt and returned to her parents' house to pick up her car keys, discovered Krissy lying face down near the front door. After failing to revive her, Niki dialed 911. "She's not breathing," she frantically told the operator. Rushed to a hospital, Krissy was pronounced dead at 5:39 a.m.

Following Krissy's mysterious death, the rumors spread quickly. Fashion insiders speculated that Taylor had been using Primatene Mist, a nonprescription asthma remedy, to get an over-the-counter high. They wondered whether she had been abusing booze or drugs. And they whispered that Krissy, like many models, must have starved herself until her body was vulnerable to any minor shock. In short, they found it difficult to accept the simple truth: Krissy was a clean-living kid whose death was accidental. It turned out she was the victim of a surprising killer: asthma. "Most people don't know that even mild asthma can cause sudden, unexpected death," said Broward County medical examiner Dr. Joshua Perper. He also concluded that the Primatene Mist that Krissy had used to relieve shortness of breath was likely not a factor in the death.

For weeks after Taylor's death, messages from her bereaved friends—"Goodnight I love you"—kept coming in on her beeper, which her mother now carries. "Krissy's physical beauty captured everyone's eye," says Barbara. "But her inner beauty is what we will remember."

GOODBYES 1995

British writer *Sir Kingsley Amis*, 73, who bitingly satirized class distinctions and social mores in more than 20 novels, from 1954's *Lucky Jim* to this year's *The Biographer's Moustache*; a month after crushing several vertebrae in a fall.

Raspy-voiced actor and comedian *Rick Aviles*, 41, whose movie credits include playing the lowlife who killed Patrick Swayze in *Ghost* (1990); of heart failure.

Director *Gilbert Moses*, 52, a cofounder in 1963 of the Free Southern Theater, an influential black touring troupe based in Jackson, Mississippi, and director of two segments of the 1977 miniseries *Roots*; of multiple myeloma.

British stage actor *Eric Porter*, 67, who played Soames Forsyte in *The Forsyte Saga*, the BBC series that became a U.S. hit via public TV in 1969; of cancer.

Composer *Miklos Rozsa*, 88, who won Oscars for *Spellbound* and *Ben-Hur*; of a stroke.

Danny Arnold, 70, an Emmy-winning TV writer-producer who created the hit series *Barney Miller* (1975-1982); of heart failure.

Actress *Viveca Lindfors*, 74, who made her screen debut in 1949's *Night Unto Night* opposite Ronald Reagan and later married its director, Don Siegel; of complications from rheumatoid arthritis.

GINGER ROGERS

Some seven decades ago, when a teenage Ginger Rogers moved up from winning a Charleston competition in Texas to the vaudeville stage in New York City, she was pleased to discover how effortlessly she was able to establish rapport with an audience. "I realized that there was a trick," she said later, "and that was being warm with them." A simple enough credo, but it carried Rogers through 73 movies, most notably the 10 unforgettable musicals (including 1938's *Carefree,* right) in which, paired with Fred Astaire, she whirled across elegant Art Deco sets trailing feathers and chiffon, setting an unmatchable standard for dancing on film. There were also her straight-shooting performances, including the working-girl heartbreaker *Kitty Foyle* (1940), for which she won an Oscar.

Personally, she preferred sports and fishing on her Oregon ranch to the showbiz whirl. She didn't drink, and she kept a soda fountain in her home instead of a bar. Her only concession to the Hollywood gossip columnists were flings with Cary Grant and Howard Hughes in the '30s, and a string of failed marriages including to comic Jack Pepper, actors Lew Ayres, Jack Briggs and Jacques Bergerac, and actor-producer William Marshall.

One recent friend was *Wings* star Crystal Bernard, who met Rogers at Bob Hope's 90th birthday party in 1993 and kept in touch until her death at age 83. Bernard called once after a bad day on the set and Rogers, to console her, recalled a similarly rough day of filming more than half a century before. "But that's just the way it is," the old star counseled. "Let it pass, and enjoy it the best you can."

ART FLEMING

Game show host Art Fleming, who died at age 70 of pancreatic cancer at his home in Crystal River, Florida, gave the answers so that contestants could ask the questions on TV's *Jeopardy!* (from the show's start in 1964 to '75, and then again from '78 to '79). Fleming, a history buff, also had roles in 48 movies, including *MacArthur* (1977).

JAMES HERRIOT

Veterinarian James Alfred Wight—who used the pen name James Herriot—was well past 50 when his wife, Joan, challenged to him to submit his stories about rural life in Yorkshire, England, to a publisher. In 1972, *All Creatures Great and Small* became an instant classic, and before his death at age 78 from prostate cancer, Herriot's books, 18 in all, sold 60 million copies worldwide and inspired two movies and a TV series. Still, success had little effect on his daily routine. "If a farmer has a sick cow," he said, "they don't want Charles Dickens turning up; they want a good vet. And that's what I've tried to be."

MICKEY MANTLE

As a New York Yankee rookie in 1951, Mantle was given a daunting buildup by manager Casey Stengel: "This guy is going to be better than Babe Ruth and Joe DiMaggio." Mantle never quite measured up to those standards, but he came close. In an 18-year career that was constantly hobbled by injuries, he hit 536 home runs and led the Yanks to seven World Series rings. Millions of boys imitated everything from his head-down run to his languid Oklahoma drawl. But he turned out to be a hero fraught with frailty.

Driven to alcoholism, he said, by a fear of early death—his father and grandfather died of Hodgkin's disease before the age of 41—Mantle could be surly and downright obscene to his adoring public. By his own admission, he also too often ignored his wife, Merlyn, and sons Mickey Jr., David, Billy and Danny. "I wasn't a good family man," he said last year, and after years of abusing his health, he entered the Betty Ford Center in 1994 for treatment of alcoholism. "From now on, Mickey Mantle is going to be a real person," he promised. He was true to his word, but 16 months later he was diagnosed with cancer and underwent a liver transplant. Then came word that the cancer had spread and was swiftly overwhelming other organs. Though some questioned whether a scarce liver had been wasted on Mantle, a public awareness campaign for which he coined the slogan—"Be a hero. Be a donor"—prompted a significant increase in the number of people requesting donor cards.

Upbeat to the end, Mantle liked to tell a story about his arrival at the Pearly Gates, where St. Peter shook his head and sent him away. Mantle turned to leave, only to be summoned back. "Before you go," St. Peter remarked, "God wants to know if you'd sign these six dozen balls."

GOODBYES 1995

Actress *Patricia Welsh*, 80, who provided the gravelly voice of the title character in *E.T. The Extra-Terrestrial*; of pneumonia.

Wall Street whiz *Jeffrey P. Beck*, 48, a mergers-and-acquisitions specialist who was nicknamed Mad Dog because he would howl after completing a profitable megadeal; of a heart attack.

Poet *James Merrill*, 68, who once described his work as "chronicles of love and loss" and won a Pulitzer in 1976 for *Divine Comedies*; of a heart attack.

British tennis champ *Fred Perry*, 85, who was the first man to win all four Grand Slam titles and in 1936 became the last Englishman to win a Wimbledon singles title; of heart failure.

Donald Pleasence, 75, the bald, beady-eyed British character actor who appeared in more than 120 films, including five of the Halloween horror series and *You Only Live Twice* (1967), in which he was James Bond's evil adversary Blofeld; while recovering from heart-valve surgery.

Colorado housewife *Virginia Tighe Morrow*, 72, who 41 years ago sparked a national debate on reincarnation after she spoke under hypnosis of a past as a 19th-century Irishwoman known as Bridey Murphy; of breast cancer.

119

GALE GORDON

Harrumph and bluster were Gale Gordon's comic calling cards, most memorably as Eve Arden's grumpy 1950s high school principal, Osgood Conklin, on *Our Miss Brooks;* as bedeviled Mr. Wilson on *Dennis the Menace* (1962–63); and (at left) as stuffed-shirt bank president Theodore J. Mooney opposite Lucille Ball on *The Lucy Show* (1962–68). The son of actors, Gordon early on mastered a slow burn that became his TV trademark, but offscreen, coworkers praised his hard-working perfectionism. When he succumbed to lung cancer at age 89, his death came just a few weeks after that of Virginia, his wife of 55 years.

BURL IVES

Poet Carl Sandburg once called him "the mightiest ballad singer of this or any other century." Burl Ives was certainly among the most traveled, whether he was hoboing across the States in the '30s or giving concerts around the globe in the '50s. He also carved an imposing presence onscreen, portraying cranky cattle barons (1958's *The Big Country,* for which he won a Best Supporting Actor Oscar) and crafty patriarchs—most notably, Big Daddy, in the 1958 film version of Tennessee Williams's *Cat on a Hot Tin Roof.* But friends remember the 6' 2", 270-lb. Ives as a gentle giant. "He possessed this wonderful, teddy-bear warmth," recalls his *Cat* costar Elizabeth Taylor. "I loved him, and I will miss him." So will generations of kids who grew up singing Ives's signature songs "Big Rock Candy Mountain" and "Blue Tail Fly."

Ives's second wife, Dorothy, whom he married in 1970, and his three stepchildren were at his bedside when he died of throat cancer at age 85. "His soul was as deep as his voice," says producer Lester Persky. "He could thunder, but never in anger, and he had an all-encompassing calm about him. He was just a great Big Daddy."

BESSIE DELANEY

Annie Elizabeth Delaney (standing) once declared, "I haven't been afraid to live, and I won't be afraid to die." When death finally came at age 104, Bessie Delany—the genteel firebrand who, with her sister Sadie, charmed readers in their feisty 1993 memoir *Having Our Say: The Delany Sisters' First 100 Years*—approached it on her own terms. Although she was the second black woman to practice as a dentist in New York State, she couldn't abide doctors or hospitals. "She got what she wanted," says Amy Hill Hearth, the journalist who cowrote *Having Our Say*. "She didn't suffer. She died in her own bed."

Bessie had been thrilled by the success of the book, which sold nearly a million copies. "Twenty-eight weeks on *The New York Times* best-seller list—not bad for two old inky-dinks!" she told Hearth. Deluged with more fan mail every week than Jerry Seinfeld and Paul Reiser combined, the sisters were unable to reply to every letter. Instead, they responded in 1994 with *The Delany Sisters' Book of Everyday Wisdom*, in which Bessie confessed, "I'm not too old to get crushes." Ever adventurous, the Delanys accepted an invitation to pose for a pantyhose ad. But fame never swayed them. Though Bessie traded one-liners with Bill Cosby (whose wife Camille coproduced a well-received Broadway version of *Having Our Say*) and kept an album of her meeting with Hillary Clinton, the maiden ladies, as they called themselves, often declined requests to receive celebrities.

Although Sadie, the first black home economics teacher in a New York City high school, often said, "I give myself two weeks without Bessie," she is "strong and doing well," reports Hearth. As always, she is, at 106, facing the future without flinching. "I'm not going to give up," she told Hearth. "I'll just do the best I can without her."

ED FLANDERS

In Emmy winner Ed Flanders's most famous moment as the quietly anguished Dr. Westphall on the classic series *St. Elsewhere* (1982–87), he defiantly flashed his derriere at the corporate owners of St. Eligius's hospital. Off-screen Flanders was tortured by alcoholism and ill health and spent his final days in a depression so deep he rarely left his sofa. He finally committed suicide, at age 60, using a Savage .30.06 rifle. His son Ian, 31—one of four children from three marriages—said afterward: "He's not in pain anymore, and for that I am at peace."

PETER COOK

"One of the ways to avoid being beaten by the system," the deadpan Brit Peter Cook once said, "is to laugh at it." Cook (6' 4") and longtime sidekick Dudley Moore (5' 2") were the Mutt and Jeff of sophisticated satire, starring on Broadway in *Good Evening* and in films like *Bedazzled* and *The Hound of the Baskervilles*. (Cook was Holmes, above). After Cook's death at 57 of gastrointestinal hemorrhaging, Moore said, "He had a verbal wit that was second to none."

ALEXANDER GODUNOV

Alexander Godunov was that quintessential Cold War creature, a star in his own country who could achieve brighter fame only by leaving it. The strapping, 6'3" dancer stunned Soviet audiences in 1971, when he made his debut at age 21 in *Swan Lake* at the Bolshoi Ballet in Moscow. Eight years later, his defection to the U.S. almost caused an international incident. And he became an object of even greater public fascination during the '80s when he and actress Jacqueline Bisset were a romantic duo of astounding leonine beauty.

When Godunov gave up dancing and made his film debut as an Amish farmer in

1985's *Witness*, critics predicted he would become a screen idol. But his movie career never took off and, riddled with self-doubt, he succumbed to the eventually fatal effects of acute alcoholism. "Alexander was his own worst critic," says Bisset, whose romance with him ended in 1988, "which sometimes rendered him fearful."

"I try to keep my feelings inside of me," Godunov once said. "I push them inward." His friends can only wonder about the loneliness he tried to live with but could not. "He was a magnificent dancer," says Svetlana Zovorotina, a Bolshoi colleague. "But who knows what went on in his soul?"

GOODBYES 1995

Pioneering publicist *Edward Bernays*, a nephew of Sigmund Freud, who lived to age 103. His client list during his 70-year career included every President from Calvin Coolidge through Dwight Eisenhower, as well as Enrico Caruso, Thomas Edison and Henry Ford.

Cheese manufacturer *Victor Dorman*, 80, who in the mid-1950s figured out how to sell sliced cheese in prepackaged form; of complications from muscular dystrophy.

Playwright *Sidney Kingsley*, 88, whose work included *Men in White* (1934), a medical drama that won the Pulitzer Prize, *Dead End* (1935), about life in the slums, and *Detective Story* (1949); of a stroke.

Comedy writer *Edward James*, 87, who created the radio version of *Father Knows Best* and whose later credits included the TV sitcoms *My Three Sons*, *The Addams Family* and *Leave It to Beaver*; of complications from emphysema.

Actor *Paul Brinegar*, 77, who dished out the grub as Wishbone, the surly chuck-wagon cook on *Rawhide* (1959-66); of emphysema.

Educator *Evelyn Wood*, 86, whose name was synonymous with speed-reading after she opened her first Evelyn Wood Reading Dynamics Institute in 1959; of heart failure.

Dr. Thomas A. Harris, 85, a psychiatrist and the author of the best-selling self-help book *I'm O.K.—You're O.K.* (1969); of a heart attack.

CHEYENNE BRANDO

Cheyenne Brando lived in a house of pain. One of 11 children sired with various women by actor Marlon Brando, she had struggled with inner demons since 1990, when her half brother Christian shot and killed her lover, Dag Drollet, the son of a Tahitian politician. After earlier suicide attempts, she hanged herself at age 25. Marlon was too emotionally devastated to join Cheyenne's mother, Tarita, a Tahitian actress, and 4-year-old Tuki, Cheyenne's son by Drollet, at the funeral.

GARY CROSBY

In his 1983 memoir, *Going My Own Way,* Gary Crosby stripped away the good-guy facade of his dad—crooner Bing Crosby—revealing a childhood of abuse. After briefly hosting his own radio show, Gary (right, with guest star Bing in 1954) went on to modest fame as a TV actor on *Adam-12* and *Hunter*. "I finally got my s--t together," Gary said two weeks before dying of lung cancer at 62. "I stopped fighting the fact that Bing Crosby was my father."

HUGH O'CONNOR

Carroll O'Connor knew that his adopted son Hugh, 32, who appeared with him on CBS's *In the Heat of the Night*, was depressed after years of drug use and "couldn't face" rehab. But nothing prepared him for the last call he got from Hugh. "He told me he was going to shoot himself," said O'Connor. Police arrived too late to intervene.

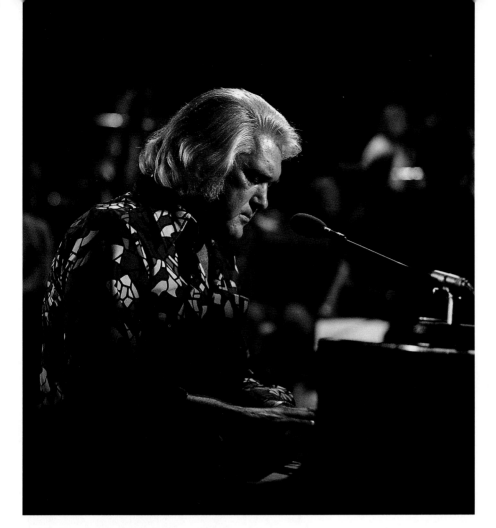

CHARLIE RICH

Dubbed the Silver Fox because of a long mane that turned prematurely white, country singer Charlie Rich was blessed with a baritone that was smooth and rivaled the soulful purity of Elvis Presley's voice. He reached his commercial peak in the early '70s with two 2-million-selling singles: "Behind Closed Doors" and "The Most Beautiful Girl." But after this burst of popularity, he mostly shunned the spotlight until his death, at 62, from a blood clot in his right lung. Rich was "a walking contradiction," his friend Kris Kristofferson once said, "partly truth and partly fiction."

He certainly experienced his share of down-home downers. Born on a farm in Colt, Arkansas, he learned the blues from cotton pickers. At age 7, he saw his brother killed by a tractor, and he hid in the woods for three days. After a brief hitch in the Air Force, he set out to make a living on his own Arkansas cotton patch while honing his music skills in private. Then in 1957, his wife, Margaret Ann, took demo tapes of his songs to Memphis, and he was invited to join the luminous roster of Sun Records. Eventually Rich, a gifted pianist and songwriter, helped create the lushly orchestrated "countrypolitan" style that came to dominate country music in the '70s. By then, however, he was often dead drunk on gin and lucky to keep from falling off the piano stool. "I think a guy who's had just the right amount of booze can sing the blues a hell of a lot better than a guy who is stone sober," he rationalized. Months before he was named Country Music Entertainer of the Year in 1974, he checked into rehab.

In recent years Rich lived in retreat with his wife at a stately home in Memphis. He resurfaced in 1992 with the album *Pictures and Paintings*, on which he sang, one critic wrote, "with the weary resignation of a lover who expects loneliness as his fate."

GOODBYES 1995

Newscaster *Frank Blair*, 79, a mainstay on NBC's *Today* show for 23 years. "The wonderful thing about Frank, whom I knew first as a viewer when I lived in South Dakota, was that he was like this uncle in your family that you could trust," says NBC's top newsman and *Today* alumnus Tom Brokaw. "He always had dignity and read the news wonderfully well."

Veteran character actor *Elisha Cook Jr.*, 91, who played Wilmer, the furious gunman baited by Humphrey Bogart's Sam Spade in *The Maltese Falcon* (1941); five years after being disabled by a stroke.

Former British prime minister *Harold Wilson*, 79, a member of the Labour party who served as head of England's government from 1964 to '70 and from '74 to '76; of Alzheimer's disease.

Animator *Isadore "Friz" Freleng*, 89, who helped create such cartoon favorites as Sylvester the Cat and Tweety Bird and won five Oscars, including one in 1964 for *Pink Phink*, starring the Pink Panther; of natural causes.

Comic actor *Severn Darden*, 65, who helped found Chicago's famous Second City improvisational troupe in 1959; of heart failure.

Guitarist *Sterling Morrison*, 53, a founding member of the pre-punk band the Velvet Underground; of non-Hodgkin's lymphoma.

PETER TOWNSEND

British Royal Air Force fighter pilot Peter Townsend's romance with Princess Margaret during the '50s titillated the United Kingdom like nothing since the abdication in 1936 of King Edward VIII. In 1955, Margaret was forced by pressure from her sister, Queen Elizabeth, and the Church of England to choose between the dashing Townsend, a divorced commoner nearly 16 years her senior, and her royal position and income. She chose the latter, escaping into London high life and winding up Fleet Street fodder. He wed Belgian heiress Marie-Luce Jamagne in 1959 and spent the years until his death of cancer at age 80 in self-imposed exile in France, where he worked as a wine buyer and a public-relations executive and wrote six books.

ALISON HARGREAVES

Among the ranks of the world's elite mountain climbers, Alison Hargreaves, 33, was one of the most audacious. Last May she became the first woman—and only the second human being—ever to reach the 29,028-foot summit of Mount Everest, the world's highest peak, solo and without using oxygen tanks. Then, just two weeks after returning home to Scotland, the restless Hargreaves left behind her husband, Jim Ballard, a photographer, and their children Tom, 6, and Kate, 4, to tackle the world's second-highest peak: K2, in the desolate Karakoram range on Pakistan's border with China.

On August 13, Hargreaves and her party of climbers announced by radio that they had reached the K2 summit. But soon afterward a storm slammed into the mountain. Six days later, other climbers spotted Alison's body not far from a staging camp at 23,302 feet. In all, seven people died and, because of the danger of recovery operations, their bodies were left on the mountain.

Back home in Scotland, Ballard greeted the news of his wife's death with resignation. "I can hear her repeating her favorite saying," he says. " 'One day as a tiger is better than a thousand as a sheep.' That sums up Alison perfectly."

HOWARD COSELL

The most celebrated and controversial sportscaster in television history, Howard Cosell was the signature voice of ABC-TV and radio sports from 1953 to 1992. And what a voice he was! Booming. Nasal. Hectoring. Straight out of Brooklyn. But during his 13 years on *Monday Night Football*, Cosell became a good deal more: a cultural icon, the man who, in his quest to "tell it like it is," brought sports into the real world by exploring such issues as drug use among athletes and racism.

Early in his career Cosell hitched his star to a rising heavyweight, Muhammad Ali (with him, above, in 1972). Ali's trainer, Angelo Dundee, speaks warmly of Cosell. "He'd say to me, 'Look at that wife of yours, she can't take her eyes off me,' " Dundee recalls. "And I'd say, 'Howard, my wife needs glasses.' " In 1967, when Ali refused to be drafted into the Army, Cosell attacked the New York State Boxing Com-

mission for stripping him of his heavyweight title. He went to bat as well for John Carlos and Tommie Smith, the Olympic sprinters who raised their fists in a black-power salute as they were awarded medals during the 1968 Summer Games in Mexico City. It hardly mattered to him that the network was deluged with hate mail.

Cosell was dealt a devastating personal blow in 1990 when he lost Emmy, his wife of 54 years, with whom he had two daughters. He died a lonely man, stricken by a heart embolism at 77. "Something about Howard that people cannot understand today," says Peter Bonventre, a former Cosell producer, "is that in the '70s and early '80s he had to be the most recognizable man in America. You couldn't walk down the street anywhere with him and not have everybody know him—kids of 5 or 6 and little old ladies. They would scream, 'Howie, tell it like it is!' "

GOODBYES 1995

Blues singer and guitarist *Ted Hawkins*, 58, whose plaintive but gutsy style earned him critical acclaim for such works as the 1982 album *Watch Your Step*; of a stroke.

Industrial designer *Brooks Stevens*, 83, who overhauled the Harley-Davidson motorcycle's look, put the sizzle in Oscar Mayer's promotional "Wienermobile," created the first widemouthed peanut butter jar, and coined the phrase "planned obsolescence"; of heart failure.

Fashion designer *Vera Maxwell*, 93, who helped pioneer sportswear for American women and counted Grace Kelly, Pat Nixon and Rosalynn Carter among her customers; of a stroke.

Philip Burton, 90, a Welsh stage director and drama teacher; of a stroke. He was so impressed during the 1940s by the talents of one of his pupils, Richard Jenkins, that he made him his legal ward. Jenkins changed his name to Richard Burton and later credited his mentor for his world-class success.

Bandleader *Les Elgart*, 76, who cowrote the 1954 instrumental "Bandstand Boogie," which became the theme song for Dick Clark's long-running *American Bandstand*; of a heart attack.

Woodcarver *Mike Kent*, 37, host of the four-year-old PBS how-to series *That Can't Be Wood!*; of cancer.

JERRY GARCIA

Bearded and gray, a middle-aged man whose weight sometimes ballooned to 300 pounds, Jerry Garcia seemed the antithesis of a rock star. Yet he was a riveting figure onstage, a benevolent Buddha whose face beamed with merriment and sometimes sorrow as crystalline notes soared and burst from the guitar that he seemed to play not with his hands, but his heart. "For me," Garcia once said about the music he performed as leader of the Grateful Dead, "it's always emotional."

The Dead scored only one Top 10 single—1987's "Touch of Grey"—in a 30-year history that produced more than 25 albums. But thanks to the communal magic of their live shows, at which graying oldsters mingled with tie-dyed teens and twenty-somethings, Garcia and the Dead enjoyed a level of success seldom equaled in pop history. And when Garcia's heart, ravaged by years of drug abuse and related health problems, finally gave out on him at age 53, his fellow musicians were stunned. "There's a lesson here," says old San Francisco pal Joe McDonald, whose band, Country Joe & the Fish, was a Dead contemporary. "It's a failure to get him to change his lifestyle. He could easily be alive today. He killed himself, make no mistake."

Until checking into a San Francisco drug rehab center shortly before his death because of a relapse into heroin addiction, Garcia seemed to have conquered his demons. Married to filmmaker Deborah Koons, 45, who encouraged him to diet and exercise, Garcia had finally grown close to his four daughters, ages 6 to 32, from two previous marriages. And he had begun work on an interactive, multimedia project tentatively titled "Jerry Garcia's Psychedelic Memoir," which was to have included samples of his art and a musical sound track. But Garcia balked at including a text about his own life. "His feeling was that writing an autobiography was premature," says his agent John Ferriter. "He had so much living to do."

In 1967, the Grateful Dead—(from left) Garcia, harmonica player Ron "Pigpen" McKernan, bassist Phil Lesh, guitarist Bob Weir and drummer Bill Kreutzmann—helped make Haight-Ashbury in San Francisco the American answer to Liverpool. The stoned '60s "were pretty weird times," recalled Garcia. "I was very, very far out."

DOUG McCLURE

Blond, beguiling and ever-smiling, Doug McClure teamed with his childhood buddy James Drury to define TV cowhand bonding on *The Virginian* (1962-71). They also hit the drinking trail hard, according to Drury, who eventually gave up booze and persuaded McClure to do the same (along with cigarettes) in 1982. McClure's drinking may well have contributed to four divorces before he settled into a 16-year union with his wife Nancy, who was with him when he died of lung cancer at age 59. "Anytime I laid eyes on Doug, I couldn't help smiling," says Drury. "He was the finest guy I ever knew."

LOUIS MALLE

From the beginning, it was an unconventional pairing. When *Murphy Brown* star Candice Bergen and film director Louis Malle met in 1979, she was 33 and beginning to wonder if she would ever meet Mr. Right. He was French, 14 years her senior, with a distinguished cinematic and romantic history (*Murmur of the Heart, Pretty Baby, Atlantic City,* Jeanne Moreau and Susan Sarandon). Yet for both Bergen and Malle, their late-blooming love was shiny and new. "With Candice, I surrendered completely for the first time in my life," Malle said. Following their marriage a year later, he continued making movies, including 1981's quirky *My Dinner With André* and 1987's Oscar-nominated *Au Revoir les Enfants,* an autobiographical story of Jewish children hidden at a Catholic boarding school in World War II France. Malle worked mostly in France and commuted to L.A. every other month to spend time with his wife and daughter, Chloe, who was born in 1985. Life was golden until Malle fought a losing nine-month battle with cancer of the lymph nodes. "Between marrying, having a child and *Murphy,* this past 10- or 15-year period has been so rich," Bergen said as she reflected on the couple's time together. "I just know enough to know that those things can't go on forever."

130

LINDA GOODMAN

For millions of Americans, the Age of Aquarius arrived with Linda Goodman. Armed with heavenly charts and a down-to-earth writing style, the astrologer alchemized the belief that the stars could forecast the future out of the realm of exotica and onto the best-seller lists. Her 1968 book *Sun Signs* sold more than 5 million copies and spawned the sequels *Love Signs* and *Star Signs*. Steve McQueen and Princess Grace as well as Sonny and Cher sought her counsel. But Goodman seemed unable to come to terms with the mysteries of her own life. After her 21-year-old daughter Sally committed suicide in 1973, Goodman refused to believe she was dead. "She contacted the FBI and the CIA," says friend Bob Slatzer. "She couldn't let it go."

In time Goodman stopped believing in death altogether and claimed Marilyn Monroe, Howard Hughes and Elvis Presley were all still alive but in hiding. After she was diagnosed in the mid-'80s with diabetes, Goodman shunned treatment and rarely left her home in Cripple Creek, Colorado. Still, she looked to the stars. *Linda Goodman's Love Signs Relationship Report*, an analysis of couples' astrological compatibility that she finished before her death at age 70, will soon hit the Internet. "Linda really did believe in love," says friend Rob Dorgan, "and she lived her life for it."

GOODBYES 1995

Saxophonist *Jr. Walker*, 64, whose bluesy style led to such '60s hits as "Shotgun" and "What Does It Take (to Win Your Love)"; of cancer.

Movie mogul *David Begelman*, 73, who was implicated in a 1970s check-forging scandal while he was president of Columbia Pictures; of a self-inflicted gunshot wound.

Former *New York Times* columnist and correspondent *James Reston*, 86, longtime dean of the Washington press corps; of cancer.

Five-time world champion Formula One race driver *Juan Manuel Fangio*, 84; of pneumonia and kidney failure.

Houston Post publisher *Oveta Culp Hobby*, 90, who headed the Women's Army Corps during WW II and was the first Secretary of Health, Education and Welfare; of a stroke.

Shakespearean actor *Sir Robert Stephens*, 64, who was in the 1969 film *The Prime of Miss Jean Brodie* with his then-wife, Maggie Smith; after a liver and kidney transplant.

Frank Hammond, 66, pioneering pro tennis umpire; of Lou Gehrig's disease.

Vivian Blaine, 74, musical comedian beloved on stage and screen as Miss Adelaide in *Guys and Dolls*; of congestive heart failure.

Legendary, luckless aviator *Douglas "Wrong Way" Corrigan*, 88, who got turned around enroute from New York to California in 1938 and landed in Ireland; from anemia.

JOHN CAMERON SWAYZE

Former anchorman John Cameron Swayze, who lived to age 89, was the voice for 20 years of Timex watches ("It takes a licking and keeps on ticking"). He began his broadcasting career on the radio in his native Kansas before joining NBC television in 1949 to host *The Camel News Caravan*. A 15-minute news program that was the forerunner of *The Huntley-Brinkley Report*, the show ran nearly eight years and made famous Swayze's authoritative yet folksy delivery and his trademark sign-off, "That's the story, glad we could get together."

J.W. FULBRIGHT

Dissent, J. William Fulbright once observed, "is an act of faith. Like medicine, the test of its value is not its taste but its effect. . . ." For those on the receiving end of the Arkansas Democrat's own eloquent dissents during his 30 years in the Senate, the taste was often bitter. Harry Truman called him "an overeducated Oxford SOB" (though he later apologized to Fulbright for any reflection on the senator's mother); Joe McCarthy vilified him as "Senator Halfbright"; and Lyndon Johnson was scathing after Fulbright, in 1966, began hearings questioning America's buildup in Vietnam. In any case, his name will live long after his death (of a stroke at 89) for the international fellowship program of which he was the legislative father.

Aloof and introspective, Fulbright was married for 53 years to Elizabeth Williams, a onetime Philadelphia socialite. A widower in 1990, he married Harriet Mayor, then director of an alumni organization for educational exchange programs. Until the end he was an inspiration to President Clinton, who served briefly on his staff in the '60s. "People dumped on our state and said we were all a bunch of backcountry hayseeds," Clinton once said. "And we had a guy in the Senate who doubled the IQ of any room he entered. It made us feel pretty good."

EAZY-E

In the end, it wasn't the gun-toting gangstas he rapped about that brought him down at 31. It was a quiet killer—a killer *without* attitude, known as AIDS. "Eazy-E, he's like the brother next door," says rapper Method Man, "and when you see it happening to him, it's time to wake up and smell the coffee."

The rapper—born Eric Wright to a retired postal worker and a school administrator—had parlayed his gritty vision of urban life into a multimillion-dollar recording empire. Starting with $25,000 he had earned dealing drugs in the crime-ridden Compton section of Los Angeles, he launched Ruthless Records, and his 1988 solo album, *Eazy-Duz-It*, went double platinum. But it was the formation of N.W.A. (Niggas with Attitude), with Dr. Dre and Ice Cube, that made gangsta rap a force to be reckoned with. The group's debut album, *Straight Outta Compton*, sold 3 million copies and angered the FBI, who complained it incited violence against police.

Wright often boasted of his sexual prowess, having fathered (and supported) eight children by seven different women. How Wright contracted AIDS is still a mystery, but he was most likely a victim of denial and misinformation. In 1991 he said, "I use condoms. I don't want to f--k around with AIDS or herpes. But in case I need it I got a big-a-- bottle of tetracycline and another gang of pills." On his deathbed, Wright wrote a cautionary message to his fans, saying he wanted "to save [them] before it's too late."

For Wright it was already too late. "It hits so close to home that it's hard for me to sleep," says L.A. rapper Rodney O. "It made me feel humble. I mean, I never had the success that Eazy had. But would I trade with him now? No."

GOODBYES 1995

Cowboy actor *John Smith*, 63, who starred on TV's *Cimarron City* (1958-59) and *Laramie* (1959-63); of cirrhosis and heart problems.

Author *Patricia Highsmith*, 74, whose psychologically rich thrillers are a staple on mystery shelves; of leukemia. Her first novel, *Strangers on a Train* (1950) became an Alfred Hitchcock classic.

Actor *Willard Waterman*, 80, star of the '50s radio and TV comedy *The Great Gildersleeve*; of bone-marrow disease.

David Wayne, 81, who won Broadway's first Tony Award for supporting actor in a musical as the leprechaun in the 1947 fantasy *Finian's Rainbow* and went on to portray the Mad Hatter in the campy '60s *Batman* TV series and the addled Dr. Amos Weatherby in the 1979-82 sitcom *House Calls*; of lung cancer.

British music hall performer *Tessie O'Shea*, 82, who won a Tony award in Noel Coward's *The Girl Who Came to Supper* (1963) and played Mrs. Hobday in the movie *Bedknobs and Broomsticks* (1971); of congestive heart failure.

Bandleader and radio personality *Phil Harris*, 89, who played a bourbon-swilling sidekick to Jack Benny from 1936 to 1952 before hosting his own program for eight years. He was the voice of Baloo the Bear in Disney's 1967 *The Jungle Book* and wed to screen queen Alice Faye; of heart failure.

IDA LUPINO

She used to joke that she was "the poor man's Bette Davis." Ida Lupino, who died of a stroke at age 77, first found fame as an actress who took on the tough-gal roles in such films as *They Drive by Night* (1940) and *High Sierra* (1941). But the culmination of her career was as a trailblazing woman director of low-budget melodramas (1953's *The Hitch-Hiker*) and TV's *The Untouchables*. In 1983, Lupino and actor Howard Duff divorced after living apart for the last 11 years of their 32-year marriage. When asked what took her so long, Lupino replied in her best wise-guy fashion: "I finally got off my duff, darling."

WILLIAM KUNSTLER

"I'm not a lawyer for hire," radical attorney William Kunstler once said. "I only defend those I love." The trial of the Chicago Seven, the motley band eventually cleared of conspiring to incite riots at the 1968 Democratic Convention in Chicago, brought Kunstler to national fame. "I believe that government is evil," he later said. "My role is always to fight it. Always be the burr under the saddle." Kunstler, who died of heart failure at 76, played himself in several films, including *The Paper* and *Malcolm X*. Since his legal work was often pro bono, those performances—and speaking engagements—helped support him. Kunstler, says his partner, Ron Kuby, always stood up "for what was right, whether it was in the face of a mob or the government or public opinion."

Fashion designer *Jean Muir*, 66, known for her superbly tailored, elegantly simple outfits; of cancer.

Glenn Burke, 42, a former outfielder with the Los Angeles Dodgers and Oakland Athletics who, in 1982, became the first major leaguer to publicly acknowledge his homosexuality; of complications from AIDS.

Author *Stanley Elkin*, 65, whose 17 darkly comic novels and collections include the highly praised *A Bad Man* (1967) and *Van Gogh's Room at Arles* (1992); of a heart attack.

Radio newscaster *Dallas Townsend*, 76, who wrote and anchored CBS radio's *World News Roundup* for 25 years; of injuries suffered in a fall.

Director *Arthur Lubin*, 96, who, between his six movies about Francis the Talking Mule and his '60s TV series *Mr. Ed*, pretty much had a lock on the gabby equine franchise; of complications from a stroke.

Screenwriter *Howard Koch*, 93; of pneumonia. He wrote radio scripts—including Orson Welles's shocking 1938 broadcast of *War of the Worlds*—and won an Oscar in 1944 for *Casablanca*, but was blacklisted in 1950, when he refused to name names before the House Un-American Activities Committee.

Ronnie White, 56, a founder of the Motown group the Miracles; of leukemia.

ORVILLE REDENBACHER

Back in the mid-'60s, farmers around Valparaiso, Indiana, thought their neighbor had lost his good sense. Cultivate expensive-to-grow "gourmet" popcorn? No way you could charge triple the going price, they maintained. Undeterred, the soft-spoken man in the bow tie went on to market superfluffy kernels that exploded into a $200 million-plus-a-year popcorn empire. More astonishing, he turned Orville Redenbacher into a household name. "We get a lot of calls from people," he once said, "who want to see if I'm for real." The answer: yes—and vigorous to the end. When Redenbacher died at 88 of a heart attack, "it came as a real shock," says his grandson Gary, 40, who had appeared in more than 100 TV commercials with him.

Popcorn's Kernel Sanders was born on a farm just outside Brazil, Indiana (pop. 7,640), in 1907. As a teenager, he once said, "I'd plant [popcorn]...and take it to the grocery store to sell it." But selling his high-end hybrid, which took 24 years to perfect, was less simple. So in 1970, after making millions producing liquid fertilizer, Redenbacher hired a Chicago marketing firm to come up with a corny sales gimmick. They did: Orville himself. Orville Redenbacher's Gourmet Popping Corn made him famous—but not superrich. He made only $350,000 when he sold his company to Hunt-Wesson Inc. in 1975. It was a deal he later regretted, but he still delighted in selling the product. "Popcorn," says son Gary, "was his passion."

HARVEY PENICK

Texas golf guru Harvey Penick was the head pro at the Austin Country Club for 48 years and tutored the likes of Tom Kite and Ben Crenshaw—not to mention duffers everywhere. In 1992, *Harvey Penick's Little Red Book,* his folksy compendium of maxims, anecdotes and tips, sold a million-plus copies. *And If You Play Golf, You're My Friend* (1993), was also a best-seller, and a third volume, *For All Who Love the Game,* was published shortly before Penick's death from pneumonia, at age 90.

MARGARET CHASE SMITH

She was the first woman to win election to both houses of Congress, but she disdained such distinctions of gender. "Isn't a woman a human being?" she once asked. "Why can't she just be a person?" During a congressional career that spanned the terms of six Presidents, she was renowned for her flinty personality, as thorny sometimes as the signature red roses she pinned to her dress each day. In 1950, as a first-term Republican senator from Maine, she was the first to denounce her colleague Joseph McCarthy on the Senate floor for his innuendo-filled crusade against alleged Communists in government. But she also had a tender side; the day after President Kennedy's assassination, she entered the Senate chamber early in the morning and laid a single rose across his old desk.

Smith, who died at 97, was guarded about her private life. For years she lived downstairs from her assistant, Bill Lewis. "Of course we loved each other," she said some time after Lewis's death in 1982. "But not like that. Looking back, I wish I would have made more time for love."

Society fixture *Jerome Zipkin*, 80, often referred to in *Women's Wear Daily* as the "social moth," a tart-tongued real estate heir who served as the confidant of such rich and famous ladies who lunch as Betsy Bloomingdale, Pat Buckley and Nancy Reagan; of lung cancer.

Sportscaster *Lindsey Nelson*, 76, known for his easygoing on-air manner as well as for the eyesore sport jackets he sought out for their loudness; of complications from Parkinson's disease and pneumonia.

Ex-Minnesota Twins shortstop *Zoilo Versalles*, 55, who in 1965 became the first Latin-American to be named the American League's most valuable player.

British-born screenwriter *Charles Bennett*, 95; of natural causes. He collaborated with Alfred Hitchcock on eight films, including *The Man Who Knew Too Much* (1934), *The 39 Steps* (1935) and *Foreign Correspondent* (1940), the last of which led to a falling-out. "[Hitchcock] loathed anybody getting any credit whatsoever," Bennett once said.

Republican *George Romney*, 88, three-term governor of Michigan during the '60s and for four years Richard Nixon's Secretary of Housing and Urban Development; of a heart attack. In 1968, Romney's presidential hopes were dashed after he said that U.S. generals had "brainwashed" him during his 1965 tour of Vietnam.

EDWARD LOWE

In the history of cats there are two dates of major significance: 1500 B.C., when the sleek little desert creatures were first given shelter inside Egyptian homes, and 1947, when they finally became proper houseguests. That was the year Edward Lowe chanced upon the cat world scent-sation he called Kitty Litter. By taming cat-box odor with clay pellets, Lowe found financial as well as olfactory success.

Forty-three years after he delivered the first hand-lettered bag of Kitty Litter to a South Bend, Indiana, pet store, he sold his company for more than $200 million. But his greatest legacy became apparent in 1985 when cats became America's favorite house pet. Today they outnumber dogs 59 million to 54 million.

Lowe's invention began with a hunch back in Cassopolis, Michigan, right after World War II. While working in his father's sawdust and clay-pellet business, the Navy veteran was visited by a friend needing sand for her cat box. He suggested she try a sack of pellets, regularly used to soak up oil spills on factory floors. The friend soon returned for another bagful, as did her neighbors.

Lowe, who died at 75 following complications from surgery for a cerebral hemorrhage, is survived by four children and second wife Darlene. Though his company had been plagued by family turmoil, in his final hours all were at his bedside, singing songs to him. "I think we didn't realize he loved us," says his daughter Marilyn Miller. "But that was all resolved at the end."

ROXIE ROKER

In her signature role in *The Jeffersons*, the long-running (1975-85), taboo-shattering Norman Lear sitcom, Roxie Roker played the chic Helen Willis in an interracial marriage (opposite Franklin Cover, left). In real life, the Shakespeare-trained Broadway actress was married at one time to white TV executive Sy Kravitz and was the mother of rocker Lenny Kravitz. Roker, who died reportedly of cancer at age 66, encouraged Lenny to be proud of his racial identity. "My mother had taught me: 'Your father's white. I'm black. You are just as much one as the other, but you are black,' " Kravitz recalled, adding, "In society, in life, you are black."

ALFRED EISENSTAEDT

Photojournalist Alfred Eisenstaedt, who lived to age 96, documented so many faces and events one almost invariably sees the century through his eyes. Among his more than 2,500 assignments for LIFE, whose staff he joined at the magazine's inception in 1936, and for PEOPLE, starting in 1974, were portraits of the world famous (Sophia Loren, right, was a favorite subject). But he has also shot ordinary folks—most memorably, the sailor and the nurse swept into a V-J Day kiss in Times Square on August 14, 1945. He credited his lifelong stamina to unstinting attention to his diet (no alcohol) and exercise (50 sit-ups and 50 push-ups a day). The mark of Eisenstaedt's genius was his total self-confidence. "The picture," he once explained, "originates in the brain." And the brain of Eisenstaedt, a native of Berlin who left Hitler's Germany in 1935, never stopped clicking. Into his 90s, he was doing portraits of such notable subjects as Hillary and Chelsea Clinton. When it came to the stars, he said, "I have photographed them all."

SERGEI GRINKOV

Sergei Grinkov and Ekaterina Gordeeva were living a fantasy on ice before his sudden death at age 28 from heart failure. Thrown together by the Soviet regime as children and told to skate for the glory of the state, they grew up to become the most celebrated pairs skaters ever—and, along the way, to fall madly in love. In the words of commentator and former skating champion Dick Button, "God gave them so much—Sergei was the perfect pairs skater, perfect husband, perfect father [to their 3-year-old daughter Daria]. It was as though God had to pull something back."

They won their first world title in 1986, when Grinkov was 19 and Gordeeva 14. Two years later, they earned their first gold medal at the Calgary Olympics. And after their marriage in 1991, they skated like no other pair had before, going on to win a second gold medal at the 1994 Olympics. Sergei and Katia kept a one-room apartment in Moscow. But they spent most of their time in Simsbury, Connecticut. Ever the romantic, Sergei gave Katia flowers frequently, and, when asked what his favorite meal was, he responded, "Any dinner my wife made." The couple was training at Lake Placid, New York, when Sergei collapsed after lifting Katia on the ice. Says former U.S. champion Rosalynn Sumners, her eyes full of tears: "How do you say goodbye to your partner? The last thing Sergei saw was Katia in her landing position, which is everything they had worked for since they were children in Moscow."

GOODBYES 1995

Malvin R. Goode, 87, an ABC reporter (1962-1973) who was the first African-American correspondent on TV network news; of a stroke.

British actor *Jeremy Brett*, 59, who played Freddy Eynsford-Hill in Hollywood's *My Fair Lady* (1964) and Sherlock Holmes in PBS's *Mystery!* series; of heart disease.

Science-fiction writer *Jack Finney*, 84, author of the 1970 cult classic *Time and Again*; of pneumonia.

Jazz singer *Phyllis Hyman*, 45, who starred on Broadway in the 1980s' Duke Ellington tribute *Sophisticated Ladies*; of an apparent suicide.

Astrophysicist *Subrahmanyan Chandrasekhar*, 84, a Nobel laureate whose research into the evolution of stars helped lead to the discovery of black holes; of a heart attack.

Fiery tennis great *Pancho Gonzalez*, 67, who won back-to-back U.S. singles titles in 1948 and 1949; of cancer.

Trumpeter *Don Cherry*, 58, who in 1959 helped launch the free jazz revolution with saxophonist Ornette Coleman; of liver failure.

Canadian novelist *Robertson Davies*, 82, author of the Deptford trilogy, who once described his central theme as "the isolation of the human spirit"; of a stroke.

Rosalind Cash, 56, a founding member of New York City's Negro Ensemble Company and a recent regular on *General Hospital*; of cancer.

ROSE KENNEDY

She was the queen mother of an American dynasty that had known both giddy triumph and crushing tragedy for the better part of a century. "Wasn't there a book about Michelangelo called *The Agony and the Ecstasy*"? Rose Kennedy once asked. "That's what my life has been like." Her father, Boston's mayor and first Irish-American congressman, was disappointed that Rose wed a saloonkeeper's son who turned out to be a philanderer. On a 1929 trip to Europe, they were joined by Gloria Swanson, Joe's mistress. Swanson wondered, wrote historian Doris Kearns Goodwin, whether Rose was "a fool, a saint or just a better actress than she was." In any case, Rose had her faith and relished the wealth and the connections, culminating in Joe's appointment as ambassador to Britain's Court of St. James's in 1937.

The Kennedys raised nine children, a roisterous royal family that was shadowed by calamity. Eldest daughter Rosemary was mentally retarded, and in 1941, without seeking Rose's approval, Joe agreed to have her lobotomized. Three years later, Joe Jr., a Navy pilot, was killed over the English Channel. Then in 1948, Kathleen, the family's golden girl, died in a plane crash in France.

On January 20, 1961, Rose stood by her son Jack as he was sworn in as President. But later that year, Joe Sr. was felled by a stroke. Then came Jack's assassination, followed, five years later, by Bobby's. And within 13 months, there was Ted's Chappaquiddick scandal. Rose remained active until she suffered a stroke in 1984. When she died, at age 104, Teddy delivered her eulogy: "She is happily presiding at a heavenly table with both of her Joes, with Jack and Kathleen, with Bobby and [grandson] David. She is home."

In 1939, the Kennedys gathered on the U.S. Embassy grounds in London (from left: Eunice, John, Rosemary, Jean, Joseph, Edward, Rose, Joseph Jr., Patricia, Robert and Kathleen).

PICTURE CREDITS

COVER (Princess Diana) Tim Rooke/Rex USA, (Courteney Cox) Scott Downie/Celebrity Photo, (Brad Pitt) Bill Davila/Retna Ltd., (George Clooney) Lisa O'Connor/Celebrity Photo, (Selena) © John Dyer 1992, (John Kennedy Jr.) Barry Talesnick/Retna Ltd., (Colin Powell) Gregory Pace/Retna Ltd. • **BACK COVER:** (Dancing Itos) Margaret Norton/NBC, (Ellen DeGeneres) Jeffery Newbury/Outline, (Deidre Hall) Deborah Feingold • **TITLE PAGE:** (Courteney Cox) Sam Jones • **CONTENTS:** (top to bottom) Miranda Shen/Celebrity Photo, Arthur Grace/Sygma, Robin Platzer/Twin Images, Magnani/Gamma Liaison, Neal Peters Collection

MOMENTS TO REMEMBER 4 (top) Gary Null/NBC, Courtesy LAPD • 5 (top) Margaret Norton/NBC, Reuters/Win McNamee/Archive Photos • 6 Jeff Kravitz • 7 Miranda Shen/Celebrity Photo • 8 Jerry Wachter/Focus On Sports • 9 (left) Gary Boas/Retna Ltd., AP/Wide World • 10 (bottom) © Louis DeLuca/Dallas Morning News/JB Pictures • 10-11 AP/Wide World • 12-13 AP/Wide World • 14 Alan S. Weiner • 15 (top) Reuters/Archive Photos, Jan Underwood/Dayton Daily News/Sygma • 16 (top right) © 1995 USA TODAY. Reprinted with permission, AP/Wide World • 17 (clockwise from top right) AP/Wide World, Dirck Halstead/Time Magazine/© Time Inc., AP/Wide World • 18-19 (clockwise from top right) Jake Hansen/London Features Intl., The Sun/Rex USA, AP/Wide World, Brooks Kraft/Sygma, David Woo/Dallas Morning News/Sygma

IN THE LIMELIGHT 20 Betty Tichich/Houston Chronicle • 21 AP/Wide World • 22 Steve Allen/Gamma Liaison • 23 Steven Ellison/Outline • 24 (top) Dana Fineman/Sygma, E.J. Camp/Outline • 25 (top) Christopher Little/Outline, Peter Serling • 26 (left) Michael Llewellyn, Jeffery Newbury/Outline • 27 (top) © 1995 Co Rentmeester, Phil Schofield • 28 (clockwise from top right) Carolyn Jones/Universal, Timothy White/Onyx, © Walt Disney Pictures • 29 (top) Tom Tavee/Atlantic Records, Karen Moskowitz/Outline • 30 (top) John Derick/Mercury Nashville, Taro Yamasaki • 31 (top) Robin Bowman, James Schnepf/Gamma Liaison • 32 (top) Steve LaBadessa, Kim Komenich • 33 (top) William Mercer McLeod, Donald Graham/Sygma • 34-35 (clockwise from top right) Reuters/Archive Photos, Roger Dong, S. Nannarello/CBS, AP/Wide World, Carlo Allegri/Agence France-Presse, Charles William Bush

TRIALS & TRIBULATIONS 36 AP/Wide World • 37 John McCoy/Los Angeles Daily News • 38 (top) AP/Wide World, David Sprague/Los Angeles Daily News • 39 (top to bottom) AP/Wide World, AP/Wide World, Pool/Agence France-Presse • 40 AP/Wide World, AP/Wide World • 41 (top) AP/Wide World, © Roger E. Sandler • 42 (left) Lisa Rose/Globe Photos, Danny Field/Shooting Star • 43 Ron Davis/Shooting Star • 44 (clockwise from top) Courtesy Reggie Doyon, Jose Juarez/Oakland Press, Paul Natkin/Outline • 45 Peattie/Sipa Press • 46 (left) Gerry Pate/Spartanburg Herald/Sygma • 47 (top) Rob Nelson/Black Star, Sygma • 48 Nina Berman/Sipa Press • 49 (left) Daniel Hulshizer, Arthur Grace/Sygma

SAVIORS & SURVIVORS 50 Charles H. Porter 4th/Sygma • 52 (left) Mark Perlstein, Bob Strong/Sipa Press • 53 Cynthia Johnson • 54 Mary Ellen Mark • 55 Ann States/Saba • 56-57 (clockwise from top right) Mark Perlstein, Thomas Renaut/Gamma Liaison, Nina Berman/Sipa Press, John Storey, Mike Guastella/Star File

WINNERS & LOSERS 58-59 Alan Singer/CBS • 60 (top) Fitzroy Barrett/Globe Photos, Ron Batzdorff/Universal • 61 (top) Brian Smith/Outline, Peter Nash • 62 (top) Robin Platzer/Twin Images, Craig Sjodin/ABC • 63 (top) Dana Fineman/Sygma, Laura D. Luongo • 64 (top) Warner Records, Edie Baskin/Onyx • 65 (top) Dorothy Low/Outline, Danny Clinch/Outline • 66 (top) West Point/Gamma Liaison, Rick Rickman/Duomo • 67 (clockwise from top) Bob Breidenbach, Jan Sonnenmair, Matthew Stockman/Allsport • 68 (both) Dale Wittner • 69 (top) Jeffrey Thurnher/Outline, AP/Wide World

PARTINGS 70 Magnani/Gamma Liaison • 72-73 (clockwise from top right) A. Savignano/Galella Ltd., Janet Gough/Celebrity Photo, Kevin Winter/DMI, E.J. Camp/Outline, John Barrett/Globe Photos • 74-75 (clockwise from top right) Steve Granitz/Retna Ltd, Ron Galella/Galella Ltd., Scott Downie/Celebrity Photo, Adam Scull/Globe Photos, Ron Galella/Galella Ltd., Steve Granitz/Retna Ltd. • 76-77 (clockwise from top right) Tony Esparza/CBS, J.A. Silva/Sygma, Brian Smale/Onyx, AP/Wide World, Red Morgan, AP/Wide World • 78-79 (clockwise from top right) Don Perdue, AP/Wide World, AP/Wide World, Robert Beck, Sam Mircovich/Reuters/Archive Photos

LOOK OF THE YEAR 80 (clockwise from top right) Nathan Bilow/Sygma, Scott Weiner/Retna Ltd., John Barrett/Globe Photos, Roger Dong • 82-83 (clockwise from top right) Steve Granitz/Retna Ltd., Alpha/Globe Photos, Jim Smeal/Galella Ltd., Jim Bourg/Gamma Liaison, UPPA/Photoreporters Inc., Sean Hahn • 84 (top) Jim Smeal/Galella Ltd., Theodore Wood/Camera Press/Globe • 85 Steve Finn/Alpha/Globe Photos

FAMILY MATTERS 86 (clockwise from top right) Richard Young/Rex USA, UK Press, Rota/Camera Press/Globe Photos • 88 (top) David Long/UK Press, Express Newspapers/Archive Photos • 89 (top) Alpha/Globe Photos • 90 (top to bottom) Walter Weissman/Globe Photos, Jim Knowles/Photofile, Brad Hahn • 91 (top to bottom) Kimberly Butler, Alistair Berg/Gamma Liaison, Marcos Corminas/Sygma • 92(top to bottom) David McGough/DMI, Neal Preston/Retna Ltd, John Johnson • 93 (top to bottom) Armen Kachaturian/Gamma Liaison, Peter C. Borsari, Time After Time • 94 (top to bottom) AP/Wide World, Alec Byrne, Sygma • 95 (top to bottom) Eika Aoshima, Gary Geiger, Alex Bailey • 96 (top to bottom) Deborah Feingold, Gary Moor, Neil Fraser/Daily Express/Archive Photos • 97 (top to bottom) Kevin Wisniewski/Silver Image, Barbara Laing/Black Star, Vladimir Sichov/Sipa Press • 98 (top to bottom) Jim Smeal/Galella Ltd., Albert Ortega/Celebrity Photo, Andrew Shawaf/Online USA Inc. • 99 (top to bottom) Volland/Borsari, Ron Davis/Shooting Star, Kevin Winter/Celebrity Photo • 100 Jan Sonnenmair • 101 (clockwise from top) Courtesy Marilyn Kane, AP/Wide World, AP/Wide World • 102 Gamma Liaison • 103 Greg Smith/Saba

TRIBUTE 104 Sung Park/Austin American Statesman/Sygma • 106-107 (clockwise from top) Larry Busacca/Retna Ltd., Jan Sonnenmair, Al Rendon/LGI, Al Rendon/LGI • 108 (top) Everett Collection, UPI/Bettmann Archive • 109 Neal Peters Collection • 110 (top) Cynthia Johnson/Gamma Liaison, Wayne Sorce • 111 Shooting Star • 112 (top) David Corio/Retna Ltd, Albert Fenn/Life Magazine/© Time Inc. • 113 D. Rubinger/Life Magazine/© Time Inc. • 114 (top) Photofest, Gerardo Somoza/Outline • 115 Barry Hollywood/Outline • 116-117 Photofest • 118 (top) Shooting Star, Express Newspapers/Archive Photos • 119 Ted Polumbaum/Life Magazine/© Time Inc. • 120 (top) Photofest, Archive Photos • 121 Marianne Barcellona • 122 (top) Globe Photos, The Kobal Collection • 123 Kenn Duncan • 124 (top to bottom) Sygma, CBS, Globe Photos • 125 David Redfern/Retna Ltd. • 126 (top) UPI/Bettmann Archive, John Paul/FSP/Gamma Liaison • 127 AP/Wide World • 128 Herb Greene/Robert Koch Gallery, S.F. • 129 William Coupon/Onyx • 130 (top) Photofest, Christopher Little/Outline • 131 Barry Staver • 132 (top) Everett Collection, Globe Photos • 133 George Rodriguez/Shooting Star • 134 (top) Lester Glassner Collection/Neal Peters, Howard Sachs/Archive Photos • 135 Thomas S. England • 136 (top) Susan Allen Sigmon, UPI/Bettmann • 137 The Detroit News • 138 (top) Everett Collection, Alfred Eisenstaedt/Life Magazine/© Time Inc. • 139 Duomo • 140-141 Dorothy Wilding

INDEX

143